KNITIVITY

KNITIVITY

CREATE YOUR OWN CHRISTMAS SCENE

FIONA GOBLE

Ivy Press

First published in the UK in 2010 by
Ivy Press
210 High Street
Lewes
East Sussex BN7 2NS
United Kingdom
www.ivypress.co.uk

British Library Cataloguing-in-Publication Data
A catalogue record for this book is available from the British Library

ISBN: 978-1-907332-45-6

Ivy Press
This book was conceived, designed, and produced by Ivy Press
Creative Director *Peter Bridgewater*
Publisher *Jason Hook*
Editorial Director *Tom Kitch*
Senior Designer *James Lawrence*
Designer *Clare Barber*
Story text *Gill Paul*
Photographer *Andrew Perris*
Illustrator *Ivan Hissey*

Printed in China

10 9 8 7 6 5 4 3 2

IMPORTANT!
Safety warning: the knitted figures are not toys. Many have small, removable parts and should be kept out of the reach of small children.

Contents

In the beginning

Knitting dolls and creatures like the ones in this book is a completely different experience from knitting clothes. And though I'm a little biased, it really is a whole lot more rewarding and entertaining. In fact, since I started making knitted dolls and creatures, I've become something of a knitting addict.

How can you compare the satisfaction of knitting a cardigan or scarf to knitting a doll with a unique look and personality, which you've created yourself?

Knitting toys is also much quicker than knitting clothes – unless you're talking about a tiny pair of mittens for a newborn baby. I promise that in this book you won't face instructions like 'continue until your work measures 50 cm (20 in)', which you know will take for ever. Your characters will start coming to life in no time.

What's more, every single one of the characters is straightforward to make. There are no fancy patterns or scary cables. If you can knit, purl, increase and decrease then you won't have any problems at all knitting the entire Knitivity cast.

Satisfaction starts here

The satisfaction starts at the very beginning, with choosing the yarns and colours for the first character in your collection.

Then, while you're knitting, you've got the excitement of seeing the character develop, often in a way that you don't expect when you begin. If you don't believe me, try knitting the Ass, or Baby Jesus and his swaddling wrap. I'm sure you'll be pleasantly surprised. When you've finished knitting your characters, you can make the manger and the fold-out stable, provided in this book, and set up your Knitivity scene. Once complete, take a step back, admire your work, and invite your family and friends to do the same.

One step at a time

If you don't fancy knitting the Knitivity in one go, why not do it in stages? In the first year, for example, you could knit Mary, Joseph, Baby Jesus and an animal or two. The year after you could add the Shepherds or Wise Men. Over a few years, you will eventually create a beautiful and detailed Knitivity that you and your family will treasure for years.

Get it together

The Knitivity also makes a great project for school groups and knitting clubs. Pool your resources of yarn, take a character each and, before you know it, your Knitivity will be complete. You may want to donate your set to a school or community group. Alternatively, it makes a great prize for a competition or Christmas raffle.

Whether you choose to create your Knitivity by yourself or with friends, I really hope you have fun and that you are as thrilled with the results as I am. But if you find yourself becoming a knitting addict, don't blame me.

Your work-box

You don't need any fancy tools to get started on your Knitivity. This is one of the best things about knitting, along with the fact that your work-in-progress is so portable. You probably have most of the tools already. Just in case you don't, the list below sets out everything you will need. In between sorting out your bits and pieces, don't forget to grab yourself a nice bag or basket to keep your project safe.

Knitting needles can be made of plastic, metal or bamboo. It doesn't matter which of these you choose, but I would recommend shorter length needles for these projects, as detailed below, because they are easier to manoeuvre. I also find it helpful when knitting small items on small needles to use ones that have fairly pointed ends.

A pair of size 3 mm (US 2/3) knitting needles
You will need these for creating the basic dolls, their clothes and the animals. This is a slightly smaller size than is usually chosen for working with double knitting (DK) yarn. This is because it is important that your knitting is tight, so that the dolls and animals keep their shape and the stuffing doesn't show through.

A pair of size 2.25 mm (US 1) knitting needles
You will need these for knitting smaller pieces, such as beards for some of the characters or ears for some of the animals.

If you knit particularly tightly or particularly loosely, you may need to choose knitting needles in a slightly larger or smaller size (see Tension on page 11).

A size 3.25 mm (US D-3) crochet hook
There's no crocheting as such involved in this book but you will need a crochet hook to make simple chains for the dolls' hair, their belts and a few other items. If you already have a crochet hook that is either a little larger or smaller than 3.25 mm (US D-3), you don't need to buy another as it will do the job perfectly well.

A pair of size 2 mm (US 0) knitting needles

You will use these for knitting the Wise Men's gifts.

A needle to sew your work together

A tapestry or darning needle is the best needle to use to sew your work together. These needles have blunt ends, which means that you will be less likely to split your yarn and spoil all your hard work.

A stitch holder or spare needle

For some of the projects, you will need something to hold spare knitting stitches while you work on another part of the knitted item. A stitch holder, which is a sort of cross between a knitting needle and a large safety pin, is specially designed for this job. But don't rush out and buy a stitch holder if you don't have one already. Because the items in this book are small, you could easily use a spare needle or an ordinary large safety pin instead.

Stitch markers

These are small plastic circles that clip easily on to your work to mark certain rows. Again, you needn't buy them especially. As a low-tech alternative, you can use small safety pins (see above right) or a short length of contrasting thread tied through the stitch.

Ordinary safety pins

Keep some of these handy. Large ones are useful for holding spare stitches while you work on another part of your knitting, and smaller ones can be used to mark up stitches in the absence of special stitch markers.

A row counter

Some people find it helpful to use a row counter to keep track of how many rows they've worked. You can get small ones that slip on to your knitting needle, others that you wear around your neck, and a variety of other models, including electronic ones. By all means, invest in one if you think it will help, but I find a pencil and paper do the job just as well.

Great yarns – and other things you need

For me, choosing the yarns I am going to use is one of the most enjoyable aspects of knitting. I love the look of the different colours lined up on the shelves of my local wool shop – from the palest pastels to dark, rich shades that gleam like jewels. I also love all the different textures of yarn you can buy, and enjoy wondering what they will look like knitted up. I even love the smell of wool shops.

Most of the yarns I recommend you use are standard double knitting (DK) yarns. These are 100 per cent wool or have a high wool content (they are often called 'natural' yarns), as opposed to the cheaper acrylic yarns. I also use standard weight gold crochet thread for several items in the Wise Men's wardrobe. I found that this knitted up perfectly on size 3 mm (US 2/3) needles.

Natural versus acrylic

Generally speaking, I prefer natural yarns to acrylic ones. This is because items made from natural yarn keep their shape better, have a bit of stretch and keep looking good for longer. Acrylic yarns, particularly the budget-priced ones, tend to produce a denser knitted fabric that can look a bit lumpy when stuffed.

On the other hand, acrylics are often available in very bright colours that are ideal for some garments in our Knitivity, such as the Wise Men's clothes and accessories. Also, there are some very funky acrylic yarns around that you will find useful for items such as the sheep's coats.

One of the downsides of natural yarn is that it is more expensive. None the less, it's really worth investing in a few balls if you want the best possible results. Because the amounts used are generally small, it's also worth going through the oddments in your knitting stash, swapping a few balls with friends or checking out the wool on sale in local thrift stores. You never know what treasures you may find.

Ultimately, the type of yarns you choose is your decision. There is absolutely no reason why you cannot use a mix of woollen and acrylic yarns for your project rather than a single type of yarn. In fact, I think your Knitivity will work best in a mixture of yarns as this will ensure your results are interesting, colourful and unique.

Getting stuffed

As well as different types of yarn, you will also need polyester toy filling. This 100% polyester filling is manufactured specially for stuffing toys and other handmade items. Check that the filling you buy is marked safe and conforms to safety standards.

Abbreviations

The following abbreviations are used in the knitting patterns in this book.

K	knit
P	purl
st(s)	stitch(es)
st st	stocking stitch
beg	beginning
k2tog	knit the next 2 stitches together
p2tog	purl the next 2 stitches together
kwise	by knitting the stitch
pwise	by purling the stitch
inc1	increase one stitch (by knitting into the same stitch twice)
m1	make one stitch (by picking up the horizontal loop lying before the next stitch and knitting into the back of it)
s1	slip one (slip a stitch on to the right-hand needle without knitting it)
psso	pass slipped stitch over (pass the slipped stitch over the stitch just knitted)
ssk	slip, slip, knit (slip 2 stitches one at a time then knit the 2 slipped stitches together)
rs	right side
ws	wrong side
alt	alternate
yfwd	yarn forward (bring your yarn from the back of your work to the front)

g	gram
oz	ounce
mm	millimetre(s)
cm	centimetre(s)
in	inches

TENSION

The general knitting tension for the patterns in this book is 12 sts and 16 rows to 4 cm (1½ in) square over st st on 3 mm (US 2/3) needles.

When knitting small items like the ones in this book, tension is not as much of an issue as it is when you are making clothes. But it is important that the knitted fabric you produce is fairly tight or your dolls and animals may look misshapen and the stuffing will show through. If your tension is significantly looser, you should choose needles a size smaller. If your tension is significantly tighter, choose needles a size larger.

Knitting essentials

The projects in this book are straightforward, quick to knit, and do not involve any complicated techniques. However, you do need to know how to cast on and cast off, both on a knit and a purl row. The only stitches you have to know are the basic knit and purl. Most of the items are knitted in stocking stitch (one row knit, one row purl) and a few of them are made in garter stitch (every row knitted).

Casting on

There are several different ways to cast on knitting. You can use whichever method you like for the projects in this book, but the one I always use is called cable casting on, and uses two needles.

1 First make a slip knot. Do this by making a loop in your wool. Then, with your knitting needle, pull a second loop of yarn through this loop. Finally, pull the knot quite tightly. This slip knot forms your first cast-on stitch.

2 To cast on more stitches, put the needle with the slip knot into your left hand. Hold the other needle in your right hand and insert the point of this needle into the slip knot and under the left needle. Wind the yarn from your ball of wool (not the yarn 'tail') around the tip of your right needle.

3 Draw the yarn through your slip stitch with the point of your right needle to form a loop.

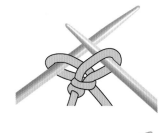

4 Now transfer the loop, which is your new stitch, on to your left needle. You will now have two stitches on your needle.

5 To make the next stitch, insert your right needle between the two stitches on the left needle and wind the yarn over the right needle from left to right.

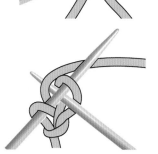

6 With your right needle, draw the yarn through the gap between the stitches to form a loop. Transfer the loop onto your left needle. You now have three cast-on stitches.

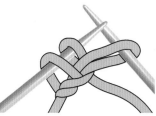

Repeat the last two steps till you have the required number of stitches on your needle.

The knit stitch

This is the most basic of knitting stitches. When you use this stitch for every row of your knitting, the stitch is called garter stitch. Garter stitch is used for some of the items in this book.

1 To make your first knit stitch, hold the needle with the cast-on stitches in your left hand. Insert the point of the right needle into the front of your first cast-on stitch.

2 Now wind your yarn round the point of your right needle, from left to right.

3 Pull the yarn through the original stitch to form a loop on your right needle. This is your new stitch.

4 Now slip the original stitch off the left needle by gently pulling your right needle to the right. Your new stitch will now be on your right needle.

Repeat these four steps till you have knitted all the stitches on your left needle. To knit the next row, transfer the needle from your right hand to your left hand.

The purl stitch

A purl stitch is like working a knit stitch backwards. Working alternate rows of knit and purl stitches creates a stitch known as stocking stitch. The purl stitches are worked with the reverse side of your work facing you while the knit stitches are worked with the front side of your work facing you. Stocking stitch is the main stitch used for the dolls, garments and accessories in this book.

1 To make your first purl stitch, hold the needle with the stitches in your left hand and make sure your yarn is to the front of your work. Insert your right needle through the front of the first stitch on your left needle, from right to left.

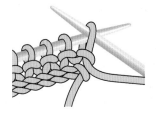

2 Now wind your yarn around the needle from right to left.

3 With the tip of your right needle, pull the yarn through the original stitch to form a loop on your right needle. This is your new stitch.

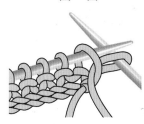

4 Now slip the original stitch off the left needle by gently pulling your right needle to the right. Your new stitch will now be on your right needle.

Repeat these four steps till you have purled all the stitches on your left needle. To work the next row, transfer the needle from your right hand to your left hand.

Casting off knitwise

When you have finished your knitting, you will need to link the stitches together to stop them from unravelling. Try not to cast off too tightly or your work will look pulled. Follow the steps below to cast off your work on the knit side of stocking stitch or on garter stitch.

1 First knit two stitches in the normal way. Then, using the point of your left needle, pick up the first stitch you knitted. Lift this stitch over the second stitch.

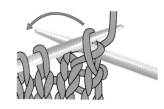

2 Knit the next stitch so you have two stitches on your needle again and repeat steps 1 and 2 until you have only one stitch left on your right needle. Cut the yarn (leaving a tail that you can use to sew your knitting together) and pull the tail through the last stitch by lifting up your right needle.

Casting off purlwise

When you are working in stocking stitch, you will sometimes need to cast off purlwise rather than knitwise, with the wrong side of your work facing you. Casting off purlwise is just like casting off knitwise, only you purl the stitches instead of knitting them.

1 First purl two stitches in the normal way. Then using the point of your left needle, pick up the first stitch. Lift this stitch over the second stitch.

2 Purl the next stitch so you have two stitches on your needle again and repeat steps 1 and 2 until you have only one stitch left on your right needle. You now need to cut the yarn (leaving a tail that you can use to sew your knitting together) and pull the tail through the last stitch by lifting up your right needle.

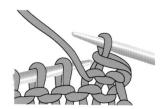

Ins and outs

Compared with bigger items like clothing, there is a lot of shaping involved in these projects, which means you need to know how to decrease and increase. There are two ways to increase the number of stitches on your needle. The first involves picking up the loop between two stitches to make another stitch. The second involves knitting into the front and back of an existing stitch.

Increasing m1

The main way to make an additional stitch is to create a new stitch between two existing stitches. In the patterns, this type of increase is written as 'm1' which is short for 'make one stitch'.

1 At the point where you want the new stitch, first pick up the horizontal loop that runs between the two stitches.

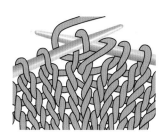

2 Next, knit into the back of it.

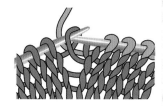

3 This creates a very neat increase.

Increasing inc 1

In some cases, you will need to increase the number of stitches in a different way. In the patterns, this type of increase is written as 'inc 1' and it is important to remember that the 'inc 1' refers to the extra stitch only. The 'second' stitch you knit is counted as an ordinary stitch. So the process explained below is actually 'inc 1, K1' (increase one stitch, knit one stitch).

For this method, begin by knitting your stitch in the normal way. But instead of sliding the old stitch off the needle, knit again through the back of it then slide it off your needle.

Decreasing k2tog & p2tog

There are a number of ways to decrease the number of stitches on your needle. The simplest way is to knit or purl two stitches together. In the patterns, these types of decreases are written as 'k2tog' or 'p2tog'.

k2tog

Put your right needle through two stitches instead of one and knit as normal.

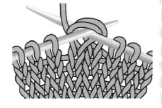

p2tog

Put your right needle through two stitches instead of one and purl as normal.

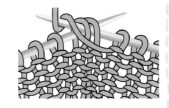

Decreasing ssk

Knitting or purling two stitches together produces a stitch that slopes to the right. This is fine in many circumstances, but when you are knitting something symmetrical you may want stitches that slope to the left. In the patterns, this type of decreasing is written as 'ssk' which is short for 'slip, slip, knit'.

First, slip one stitch and then the next stitch on to your right-hand needle, as if you were knitting them. Then insert the left-hand needle through the front loops of both these stitches and then knit them in the usual way.

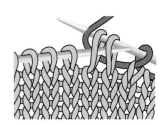

Decreasing s1, k2tog, psso

In a few cases, you will need to decrease two stitches at a time. In the patterns, this decrease is written as 's1, k2tog, psso'. This is short for 'slip one, knit two together, and pass slipped stitch over'.

1 Slip a stitch from your left-hand to your right-hand needle. Then knit two stitches together.

2 Pass the slipped stitch over the stitch you have just created.

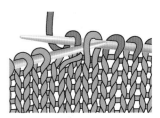

Putting it all together

Stitching pieces together neatly is one of the most important tasks in any knitting project. Get it right and your work will look professional. Rush it, and the results could be disappointing. In most cases, you should sew the pieces together using the same yarn you used for knitting. But if you have used a specialist yarn, you will find it easier to sew pieces together using a standard double knitting yarn in the same colour.

Mattress stitch

For vertical edges, such as arms, the sides of bodies, and the sides and arm sleeves of the dresses and robes, or horizontal edges such as the shoulders of the dolls' garments, I recommend using a stitch called mattress stitch, which is almost invisible.

Vertical edges

To join two vertical edges, place your two pieces side by side. Take your yarn under the running stitch between the first two stitches on one side then under the corresponding running stitch between the first two stitches on the other side.

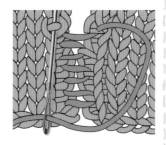

Horizontal edges

To join two horizontal edges, take your needle under the two 'legs' of the last row of stitches on one piece of knitting, then under the two 'legs' of the corresponding stitch on the other piece of knitting.

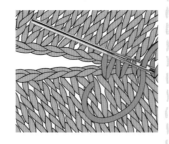

You can use mattress stitch on garter stitch, too. Because items knitted in garter stitch are denser, you need only pick up the running stitches in every other row.

Weaving stitch

To join the vertical edge of a piece of knitting to the horizontal edge of another piece, you can use a technique called weaving.

Take your needle out at a stitch on the horizontal piece of knitting, under a running stitch on the vertical piece, then back down through the original stitch. Bring your needle out through the next stitch on the horizontal piece and repeat the process. Because the width and length of stitches do not match perfectly, every few stitches you will need to take your needle through two of the running stitches of the vertical piece.

Back stitch & overcast stitch

For seaming very small items or items with curved edges, such as the dolls' heads, I recommend that you use either back stitch or overcast stitch (also known as oversewing).

To back stitch, take your needle one stitch width back from your starting point and down through your knitting. Then take your needle from the back to the front of your work one stitch width in front of your starting point.

To overcast stitch, simply take your yarn from the front over the edge of your seam and out through the front again. This technique is also useful for sewing on small items such as the dolls' arms and the animals' ears.

Other techniques

There are some other useful techniques that you will need to create the characters in this book and ensure your work looks professional. You may already have your own way of approaching these techniques. If so, please stick to your usual way of doing things. If there are any you are not sure about, this section will guide you through them.

Picking up stitches along a vertical edge

For some of the projects, you will need to pick up stitches along a vertical edge of your knitting. This is usually referred to as 'pick up and knit'.

With the right side of your work towards you, insert your needle between the running threads of the first two stitches. Then wind your yarn around your needle and pull the new loop through.

Remember that sometimes you may find that you have more running threads than the number of stitches you need; if so you will need to miss a running thread every few stitches.

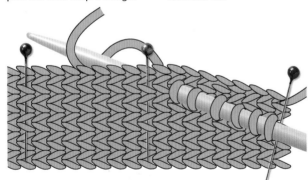

Weaving in ends

There are several ways of doing this. If possible, I try to weave the edges into the wrong side of a seam so I know they will be invisible. I find the ends are more likely to stay in place if I take my needle between the yarn's strands. If the item does not have a seam, I usually weave the ends up the side then take my yarn tail back down for a couple of stitches to ensure it stays put.

Concealing your yarn when sewing features

To take your yarn to the point where you want to sew the feature, first make a knot at one end. Next, take your needle between stitches in an inconspicuous area and out at your starting point. The knot will be embedded somewhere in your item and your thread will be secure.

Once you have finished the feature, take your needle back out through your work in an inconspicuous area. Work a couple of stitches, one on top of the other, in the running stitches between the knitted stitches (these will be slightly sunken). Then pull your yarn out somewhere else on your item and trim closely. If you squash the item a bit before doing this, the yarn end will be completely concealed when the item springs back into shape. But take care not to snip your knitting by mistake.

French knot

This embroidery technique (sometimes called a French dot or a knotted stitch) is used for the dolls' and animals' eyes and Jesus's hair.

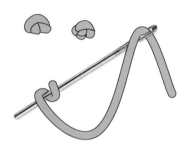

To make a French knot, use a fairly short piece of yarn to make your work easier. Bring the yarn up at your starting point. With your needle fairly near the surface of your work, wind the yarn around the needle once (or twice if you prefer the eyes a little larger). Then take the tip of your needle back into your knitting, just to the side of your starting point. It is important you don't take your needle back into the exact starting point or your knot will slip right through your knitting. Continue pulling your needle through your work and slide the knot off the needle and on to your knitting.

Chain stitch

This embroidery stitch is used for the markings on the Ass's back (see pages 40–1).

First, take your needle out at the starting point for your stitch. Now take your needle back into your knitting, just next to your starting point, remembering not to pull the yarn too tightly so there is a little loop of yarn. Then bring your needle back up through your fabric a stitch width along and catch in the loop. Pull your thread up so it is firm but not too tight.

Crochet a chain

Simple crochet chains are used for some of the dolls' hair, some of the animals' tails and a few other items such as the Wise Men's belts and the Angel's hairband.

1 To make a crochet chain, first form a slip knot on your crochet hook, as if you were starting to cast on some stitches for knitting. This is your first stitch in the chain. Holding the slip stitch on your hook, pass the yarn around the back of the hook and then to the front, so the yarn is caught in the slot of the hook as shown.

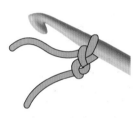

2 Draw the yarn through the loop already on your hook to form the second stitch in the chain, as shown.

Continue making the chain until it is as long as you need.

Crochet a chain border

This is used as a trimming for the scarf of one of the Wise Men and it is very easy once you get the hang of it.

To make the border, insert your crochet hook between the running threads of the first two stitches along the edge of your knitting. Then wind your yarn around your hook and pull the new loop through. Use this loop to make a chain, as described above. Next, insert your crochet hook through your knitting a little way along, pick up the yarn with your hook and pull the yarn through your knitting to form a second loop. Take the yarn around the back and over your hook again. Now use the hook to pull the yarn through the two loops on your hook. Continue in this way until you have finished the border, taking care to space your stitches evenly.

Basic standing doll

You will need to knit either a standing or a traditional-style doll (see pages 22–3) to create each of the adult figures in the book: Mary, Joseph, the Angel, the two Shepherds and the three Wise Men. The body of the Basic Standing Doll is bottle shaped, which enables the doll to stand up independently. The Traditional Doll has separate legs and so is less suited as a character in a Knitivity scene. For this reason, all the dolls shown in this book have been knitted as standing dolls, except for one version of Mary (shown on page 24).

However, it is really up to you whether you knit your dolls as standing or traditional-style dolls – or perhaps a mix of the two. The clothes for all the characters are designed to fit both basic shapes.

THE STANDING DOLL IS APPROXIMATELY 15 CM (6 IN) TALL.

Front

The front of the doll is worked as one piece, from the tip of the feet to the top of the head.

- Cast on 5 sts for the first foot.
  - Work 6 rows in st st, beg with a K row.
  - Break yarn and leave sts on the needle.
  - On the same needle, cast on 5 sts for the second foot.
- Work 6 rows in st st on these sts only, beg with a K row.
- * Next row: K5 sts across second foot, cast on 5 sts, K5 sts across first foot. [15 sts]
- Next row: P.
- ** Work 8 rows in st st, beg with a K row.
- *** Next row: K1, k2tog, K to last 3 sts, ssk, K1. [13 sts]

- Work 7 rows in st st, beg with a P row.
- Next row: K1, k2tog, K to last 3 sts, ssk, K1. [11 sts]
- Work 23 rows in st st, beg with a P row.
- Next row: K1, k2tog, K to last 3 sts, ssk, K1. [9 sts]
- Next row: P.
- Next row: K2, m1, K1, m1, K to last 3 sts, m1, K1, m1, K2.
- Next row: P.
- Repeat last 2 rows once more. [17 sts]
- Next row: K2, m1, K to last 2 sts, m1, K2. [19 sts]
- Next row: P.
- Next row: k2tog, K2, (k2tog) twice, K3, (ssk) twice, K2, ssk. [13 sts]
- Next row: p2tog, P to last 2 sts, p2tog. [11 sts]
- Next row: (k2tog) twice, k3, (ssk) twice. [7 sts]
- Next row: p2tog, P3, p2tog.
- Cast off remaining 5 sts firmly.

Back

The back of the doll is worked as one piece, from the base to the top of the head.

- Cast on 15 sts.
- Work 2 rows in st st, beg with a K row.
- Continue as front from ** to end.

Base

- Cast on 5 sts for the first foot.
- Work 6 rows in st st, beg with a K row.
- Break yarn and leave sts on the needle.
- On the same needle, cast on 5 sts for the second foot.
- Work 6 rows in st st on these sts only, beg with a K row.
- * Next row: K5 sts across second foot, cast on 3 sts, K5 sts across first foot. [13 sts]
- Work 5 rows in st st, beg with a P row.
- Next row: k2tog, K to last 2 sts, ssk.
- Next row: P.

- Repeat last 2 rows once more. [9 sts]
- Next row: k2tog, K to last 2 sts, ssk.
- Next row: p2tog, P to last 2 sts, p2tog.
- Cast off remaining 5 sts.

Arms

Make 2 identical pieces. Each arm is knitted as one piece from the top of the arm to the tip of the hand.

- Cast on 7 sts.
- Work 24 rows in st st, beg with a K row.
- Next row: K1, k2tog, K1, ssk, K1. [5 sts]
- Cast off pwise.

To make up the basic standing doll

Join the doll pieces at the sides and around the head. Stuff the doll, using a small piece of stuffing at a time. Don't stuff the doll too firmly – it should feel fairly squashy.

Place the feet of the base and the feet of the doll front right sides together and seam around the edges using back stitch (see page 17). Turn the feet the right way out so that the base is in its final position. Join the remainder of the base to the main part of the doll by taking your yarn under a loop near the edge of the base then under a horizontal loop on the first row of the main part of the doll. This technique is similar to mattress stitch (see page 17) and will form a neat, professional finish.

Seam the long edges of the arms together using mattress stitch and oversew the arm tops in place at either side of the body so that the top of the arms are about 1 cm (⅜ in) below the doll's neck.

Traditional doll

You can knit a traditional-style doll instead of a Basic Standing Doll (see pages 20–1) for each of the adult figures in the book. The body of the Traditional Doll has separate legs so it cannot stand without support (see page 79). The Basic Standing Doll is bottle shaped, which enables it to stand up independently.

THE TRADITIONAL DOLL IS APPROXIMATELY 15 CM (6 IN) TALL.

Front

The front of the doll is worked as one piece, from the tip of the feet to the top of the head. Both the front and back part of the legs are initially knitted as part of the front part of the doll. This will become clear when you start on the back of the doll.

- Cast on 12 sts for the first leg.
- Work 28 rows in st st, beg with a K row.
- Break yarn and leave sts on a stitch holder or spare needle.
- Cast on another 12 sts for the second leg.
- Work 28 rows in st st, beg with a K row.
- Break yarn.
- Leave first 6 sts of second leg on a safety pin.
- With the right side of the work facing you, rejoin yarn and K next 6 sts of second leg, K first 6 sts of first leg and leave last 6 sts on a second safety pin. [12 sts]
- * Next row: P5, p2tog, P5. [11 sts]
- Work 14 rows in st st, beg with a K row.
- Next row: K1, k2tog, K to last 3 sts, ssk, K1. [9 sts]
- Next row: P.
- Next row: K2, m1, K1, m1, K to last 3 sts, m1, K1, m1, K2. [13 sts]
- Next row: P.
- Repeat last 2 rows once more. [17 sts]
- Next row: K2, m1, K to last 2 sts, m1, K2. [19 sts]
- Next row: P.
- Next row: k2tog, K2, (k2tog) twice, K3, (ssk) twice, K2, ssk. [13 sts]
- Next row: p2tog, P to last 2 sts, p2tog. [11 sts]
- Next row: (k2tog) twice, K3, (ssk) twice. [7 sts]
- Next row: p2tog, P3, p2tog.
- Cast off remaining 5 sts firmly.

Back

- With the right side of your work facing you, rejoin your yarn at the inner edge of the stitches on the left-hand side.
- K 6 sts from the safety pin, then K 6 sts from the second safety pin, starting at the outside edge.
- Continue as front from * to end.

Arms

Make 2 identical pieces. Each arm is knitted as one piece from the top of the arm to the tip of the hand.

- Cast on 7 sts.
- Work 24 in rows in st st, beg with a K row.
- Next row: K1, k2tog, K1, ssk, K1. [5 sts]
- Cast off pwise.

To make up the traditional doll

Join the doll pieces at the inner legs, one side and around the head. Leave the second side open for stuffing. Stuff the doll, using a small piece of stuffing at a time. Don't stuff the doll too firmly – it should feel fairly squashy. Join the second side.

Seam the long edges of the arms together using mattress stitch (see page 17) and oversew the arm tops in place at either side of the body so that the top of the arms are about 1 cm (⅜ in) below the doll's neck.

The Angel Gabriel Visits Mary

More than two thousand years ago, in a little town called Nazareth, a young woman called Mary was engaged to a man named Joseph, who was a carpenter. They decided they would get married in a year's time, but until then Mary would stay in her father's house.

One night, as she was going to bed, Mary was visited by an angel called Gabriel, who was dressed in shimmering white robes. At first she was very scared and wanted to run away, but Gabriel began to speak to her in a beautiful voice and that made her feel calm.

Gabriel told Mary that she was going to have a baby son, and that she should call him Jesus. That was enough of a surprise but then he said something even stranger.

"*The holy child you give birth to will be the Son of God,*" he said. Then he disappeared.

Mary was amazed! She was just an ordinary girl, but she had been chosen to be the mother of the Son of God. She felt very proud. Then she started to worry about what Joseph would say. Would he mind?

She didn't have to worry, because Joseph already knew about the baby from a dream. In his dream, Joseph was told that this would be a very special child who would save all the people on earth from their sins.

Joseph hugged Mary and said, "*This is great news. We will have this baby and bring him up together and we will call him Jesus, just as the angel said.*"

And so they got married and Mary moved into Joseph's house, and they looked forward to the birth of their special son.

Mary

Mary is almost always shown in subtle shades of blue and white. I don't think she'd look quite like Mary in any other colours. So now's the time to pick through all those shades of blue in your knitting stash or wool shop, and find some shades that work really well together.

You will need

FOR THE DOLL

20 g (¾ oz) of dark beige DK yarn

Small amounts of black and red DK yarn for the features

A small amount of dark yellow DK yarn for the hair

A small amount of bright pink DK yarn for the sandals

15 g (½ oz) of polyester toy stuffing

FOR THE CLOTHES

20 g (¾ oz) of pale blue DK yarn

20 g (¾ oz) of mid-blue DK yarn

10 g (¼–½ oz) of white DK yarn

A small white button and a small amount of red thread for the dress

A 13-cm (5¼-in) length of gold cord for the halo and some gold or invisible thread for sewing it on

EQUIPMENT

A pair of 3 mm (US 2/3) knitting needles

A size 3.25 mm (US D-3) crochet hook

A yarn needle to sew the figure and clothes together

Doll

Using the dark beige yarn, knit, make up and stuff the basic figure as described on pages 20–1.

Using the black yarn, make two French knots for the eyes.

Untwist a short piece of red yarn into two even strands. Using one of the strands, embroider a 'V' shape for the mouth.

For the hair, use the crochet hook and dark yellow yarn to crochet three chains (see page 19); each row should be 15 cm (6 in) long. Thread the yarn at the ends of the chains back into each chain and trim. Using a separated strand of the same yarn, join the centre of the group of chains to the top of the head, about 7 mm (¼ in) to the front of the seam. Join the strands again at both sides of the head, about two-thirds of the way down the head.

To make Mary's sandals, sew a large cross stitch on the top of each foot using the bright pink yarn.

Dress

Make 2 identical pieces for the front and back. The dress pieces are knitted from the bottom to the top (neck) edge.

- Cast on 22 sts in mid-blue.
- K 4 rows then break yarn.
- Join pale blue yarn and work 4 rows st st, beg with a K row.
- Next row: K2, k2tog, K to last 4 sts, ssk, K2.
- Next row: P.
- Repeat last 2 rows three times more. [14 sts]
- Work 16 rows in st st, beg with a K row.
- Mark beg and end of last row with a piece of contrasting yarn or thread.
- Work 8 rows in st st, beg with a K row.
- Next row: Cast off 2 sts, K to end.
- Next row: Cast off 2 sts pwise, P to end. [10 sts]
- Work 4 rows in st st, beg with a K row.
- Cast off loosely.

Seam the dress pieces together along the neck edges and shoulders.

Attaching the hair

join here

and here

and here

Attaching the sleeves (see overleaf)

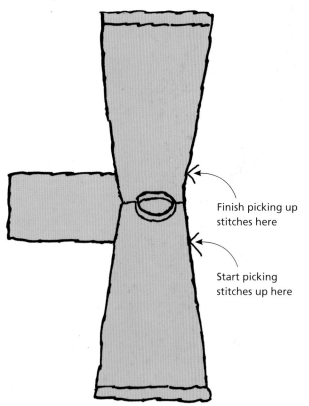

Finish picking up stitches here

Start picking stitches up here

For the sleeves, spread the two dress pieces apart. With the right side of your work facing you, pick up and K 14 sts between the two thread markers on one side of the dress.

- **Work 17 rows in st st, beg with a P row.**
- **K 2 rows.**
- **Cast off loosely.**

Complete the second sleeve in exactly the same way. Remove the thread markers.

To make up, join the underarm and side seams. Sew the button in place using red thread.

Veil

The veil is knitted from the top (forehead edge) to the bottom.

- **Cast on 10 sts in white.**
- **K 2 rows.**
- **Work 6 rows in st st, beg with a K row.**
- **Next row: Cast on 4 sts, K to end.**
- **Next row: Cast on 4 sts, P to end. [18 sts]**
- **Next row: K.**
- **Next row: P.**
- **Next row: K.**
- **Next row: K2, P to last 2 sts, K2.**
- **Repeat last 2 rows twice more.**
- **Next row: K4, k2tog, K6, ssk, K4. [16 sts]**
- **Next row: K2, P to last 2 sts, K2.**
- **Next row: K4, k2tog, K4, ssk, K4. [14 sts]**
- **Next row: K2, P to last 2 sts, K2.**
- **Next row: K2, (m1, K2) 6 times. [20 sts]**
- **Next row: K2, P to last 2 sts, K2.**
- **Next row: K.**
- **Repeat last 2 rows three times more.**
- **K 3 rows.**
- **Cast off loosely.**

To make up, join the two seams to shape the top part of the veil. The sides of the small square at the beginning of your work that will form the top of the veil should be seamed around the corner of the main part of the veil to form a hat shape.

Making up the veil

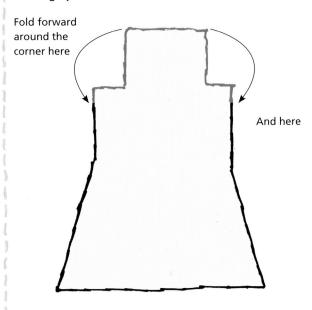

Fold forward around the corner here

And here

Sew along here

And here

Cape

The cape is knitted as one piece, from the neck edge to the lower edge.

- Cast on 24 sts in mid-blue, leaving a long tail of yarn for making one of the ties for the cape.
- K 2 rows.
- Next row: K5, inc 1 into next 2 sts, K10, inc 1 into next 2 sts, K5.
- Next row and every ws row: K2, P to last 2 sts, K2.
- Next rs row: K6, inc 1 into next 2 sts, K12, inc 1 into next 2 sts, K6.
- Next rs row: K7, inc 1 into next 2 sts, K14, inc 1 into next 2 sts, K7.
- Next rs row: K8, inc 1 into next 2 sts, K16, inc 1 into next 2 sts, K8.
- Next rs row: K9, inc 1 into next 2 sts, K18, inc 1 into next 2 sts, K9.
- Next rs row: K10, inc 1 into next 2 sts, K20, inc 1 into next 2 sts, K10.
- Next rs row: K11, inc 1 into next 2 sts, K22, inc 1 into next 2 sts, K11. [52 sts]
- Next row: K2, P to last 2 sts, K2.
- Next row: K.
- Next row: K2, P to last 2 sts, K2.
- Repeat last 2 rows once more.
- K 2 rows.
- Cast off loosely.

To make up, use the tail at the neck edge and the crochet hook to crochet a 4-cm (1½-in) chain (see page 19) for one of the cape ties. Work a matching chain for the tie on the other side and attach it. Thread the yarn at the ends of the chains back into each chain and trim.

Halo

Make a circle from the gold cord, overlapping the ends by 1 cm (⅜ in). Sew on to the back of the headdress with invisible or gold thread.

The Journey to Bethlehem

In those days, the land where Mary and Joseph lived was ruled by the Romans. One day, when Mary was heavily pregnant, the Roman Emperor Augustus issued a decree. He said that everyone had to return to the place where their families came from so that they could be counted in a census.

Mary and Joseph were horrified. Joseph's family came from Bethlehem, which was nearly eighty miles away, and it would take several days to get there. Joseph had to go because it was the law, but he couldn't leave Mary behind because the baby was due to be born any day. They had no choice. Joseph borrowed a donkey for Mary to ride, they packed a few things into a bundle and set out.

The road to Bethlehem wound through steep, rocky mountains where wolves roamed. Joseph walked along beside the donkey and they travelled all day then lay down on the hard ground to sleep at night. Day followed night, and night followed day, and they became more and more tired. One night it rained and their clothes got soaking wet. Mary started to feel very ill and her back hurt from sitting on the donkey all day. Joseph's feet were sore and he worried that they would never get there, but he said to Mary, *"Don't worry. You know that the Lord will protect us."*

After twelve days, they reached the top of a ridge and saw ahead the golden rooftops and spires of a city called Jerusalem, which was near Bethlehem. That's when they knew they were nearly there.

"Not long now, Mary," Joseph said.

Mary gave a little cry. She had a pain in her stomach. *"Oh Joseph,"* she cried in alarm. *"I think the baby is coming."*

Joseph

In his homespun clothes and brown work boots, Joseph looks every inch the carpenter. I decided to knit him in traditional shades but there is no reason why you couldn't choose a different colour scheme – particularly if those are the shades you've got spare in your work-box.

You will need

FOR THE DOLL

A small amount of brown DK yarn
for the boots

20 g (¾ oz) of pale beige DK yarn

A small amount of dark brown DK yarn
for the hair

Small amounts of black and red DK yarn
for the features

15 g (½ oz) of polyester toy stuffing

FOR THE CLOTHES

20 g (¾ oz) of lime green DK yarn

A small amount of brown DK yarn

10 g (¼–½ oz) of orange DK yarn

10 g (¼–½ oz) of flecked green DK yarn

A 13-cm (5¼-in) length of gold cord
for the halo and some gold or invisible thread
for sewing it on

EQUIPMENT

A pair of 3 mm (US 2/3) knitting needles

A size 3.25 mm (US D-3) crochet hook

A yarn needle to sew the figure and
clothes together

Front

The front of the doll is worked as one piece, from the tip of the feet to the top of the head. The boots are knitted as an integral part of the doll.

- Cast on 5 sts in brown for the first boot.
- Work 6 rows in st st, beg with a K row.
- Break yarn and leave sts on the needle.
- On the same needle, cast on 5 sts for the second boot.
- Work 6 rows in st st on these sts only, beg with a K row.
- Next row: K5 sts across second boot, cast on 5 sts, K5 sts across first boot. [15 sts]
- Next row: P.
- Work 8 rows in st st, beg with a K row.
- Break yarn and join beige yarn. Continue working as for the front of the standing doll in the normal way, starting at *** on the pattern for the standing doll on page 20.

Back

The back of the doll is worked as one piece, from the base to the top of the head.

- Cast on 15 sts in brown.
- Work 10 rows in st st, beg with a K row.
- Break yarn and join beige yarn. Continue working as for the front of the Basic Standing Doll in the normal way, starting at *** on the pattern on page 20.

Base

Work as for the base of the Basic Standing Doll (see pages 20–1) but in brown. Make up and stuff the doll as described on page 21.

Using the black yarn, make two French knots for the eyes.

Untwist a short piece of red yarn into two even strands. Using one of the strands, embroider a 'V' shape for the mouth.

For the hair, use the crochet hook and dark brown yarn to crochet a chain (see page 19), 24 cm (9½ in) long. Starting at the mid-point on one side of the head, sew the chain around the chin area to make the beard, right around the face to the starting point. Sew it across to the other side of the face to form the moustache, and around the top of the head again to the starting point to form a second layer for the hair.

Tunic

Make 2 identical pieces for the front and back. The tunic pieces are knitted from the bottom to the top (neck) edge.

- Cast on 22 sts in lime green.
- K 4 rows.
- Work 4 rows in st st, beg with a K row.
- Join brown yarn and work 2 rows in st st, beg with a K row.
- Break yarn and continue working in lime green.
- Work 2 rows in st st, beg with a K row.
- Next row: K2, k2tog, K to last 4 sts, ssk, K2.
- Next row: P.
- Next row: K.
- Next row: P.
- Repeat last 4 rows twice more. [16 sts]
- Work 8 rows in st st, beg with a K row.
- Mark beg and end of last row with a piece of contrasting yarn or thread.
- Work another 9 rows in st st, beg with a K row.
- Next row: K.
- Next row: Cast off 2 sts, K to end.
- Repeat last row once more. [12 sts]
- Cast off.

Seam the tunic pieces together 2 sts along at each side of the neck opening to form the shoulder seams.

For the sleeves, spread the two tunic pieces apart. With the right side of your work facing you, pick up and K 16 sts between the two thread markers.

- Work 15 rows in st st, beg with a P row.
- K 2 rows.
- Cast off loosely.

Complete the second sleeve in exactly the same way. Remove the thread markers.

To make up, join the underarm and side seams.

Waistcoat

The waistcoat is knitted in one piece.

- Cast on 18 sts in orange.
- K 8 rows.
- Next row: K2, k2tog, K to last 4 sts, k2tog, K2.
- K 7 rows.
- Repeat last 8 rows twice more. [12 sts]
- K 8 rows.
- Next row: K3, cast off 6 sts, K3 (including st on needle after cast-off).
- Working on last 3 sts only, K 5 rows.
- Next row: K1, inc 1 into next st, K to end.
- K 5 rows.
- Next row: K1, inc 1 into next st, K to end.
- K 3 rows.
- Next row: K to last 2 sts, inc 1 into next st, K to end.
- Next row: K.
- Next row: K1, inc 1 into next st, K to end.

- K 5 rows.
- Next row: K to last 2 sts, inc 1 into next st, K to end.
- K 7 rows.
- Repeat last 8 rows once more. [9 sts]
- Cast off.
- With the wrong side of your work facing you, rejoin yarn to neck edge of second set of 3 sts, K to end.
- K 4 rows.
- Next row: K1, inc 1 into next st, K to end.
- K 5 rows.
- Next row: K to last 2 sts, inc 1 into next st, K to end.
- K 3 rows.
- Next row: K1, inc 1 into next st, K to end.
- Next row: K.
- Next row: K to last 2 sts, inc 1 into next st, K to end.
- K 5 rows.
- Next row: K1, inc 1 into next st, K to end.
- K 7 rows.
- Repeat last 8 rows once more. [9 sts]
- Cast off.

To make up, join the side seams of the waistcoat, leaving an opening at the top for the armholes.

Headdress

The headdress is knitted from the top (forehead edge) to the bottom.

- Cast on 10 sts in flecked green.
- K 2 rows.
- Work 6 rows in st st, beg with a K row.
- Next row: Cast on 4 sts, K to end.
- Next row: Cast on 4 sts, P to end. [18 sts]
- Next row: K.
- Next row: P.
- Next row: K.
- Next row: K2, P to last 2 sts, K2.
- Repeat last 2 rows twice more.
- Next row: K4, k2tog, K6, ssk, K4. [16 sts]
- Next row: K2, P to last 2 sts, K2.
- Next row: K4, k2tog, K4, ssk, K4. [14 sts]
- Next row: K2, P to last 2 sts, K2.
- Next row: K2, (m1, K2) 6 times. [20 sts]
- Next row: K2, P to last 2 sts, K2.
- Next row: K.
- Repeat last 2 rows five times more.
- K 3 rows.
- Cast off loosely.

To make up, join the two seams to shape the top part of the headdress. The sides of the small square at the beginning of your work that will form the top of the headdress should be seamed around the corner of the main part of the headdress to form a hat shape.

Halo

Make a circle from the gold cord, overlapping the ends by 1 cm (⅜ in). Sew on to the back of the headdress with invisible or gold thread.

No Room at the Inn

It was dark when Mary and Joseph reached the walls of Bethlehem and they were puzzled to see that the streets of the town were full of people. Why was it so busy? Mary kept getting pains in her stomach and she knew it would not be long before the baby arrived.

"I'll find us a room at an inn for travellers," Joseph told her.

Mary thought to herself: "Surely the Son of God should be born in a holy temple?" But she decided to wait and see what happened.

Joseph knocked on the door of the first inn and asked, "Do you have a room?"

"No, sorry," the innkeeper said. "The whole town is full because of all the people who have come for the census."

Joseph tried another inn. "Please could you try to squeeze us in? My wife is about to have a baby."

"I'm sorry, I can't help you," the innkeeper said. "All our rooms are taken and I can't ask anyone to leave."

Joseph was panicking by the time he got to the last inn. The innkeeper looked at Mary, who was clutching her stomach in pain, and he took pity on them. "All I have is a stable out at the back," he said. "There are sheep and oxen and asses in there but at least it will keep you dry."

Mary and Joseph went round to the stable, which was small and not very clean. Was this really where the holy child would have to be born? But there was nothing else they could do, so Joseph made a bed out of hay and Mary lay down on it.

"Now go outside and build a fire," Mary said to him. "Don't worry about me. I'll be fine."

Ox

Solid and burly, the oxen usually hide in the background of a traditional Nativity scene. But I think you'll agree that this ox deserves a stage of his own. Once you've knitted him, you're bound to fall in love. I chose a smooth rich natural brown yarn for his coat that suits him perfectly.

THE OX IS 9 CM (3½ IN) HIGH AND 16 CM (6¼ IN) LONG.

Body

The body and head are knitted as one piece.

- Cast on 27 sts in dark brown.
- Work 4 rows st st, beg with a K row.
- Next row: K9, m1, K to last 9 sts, m1, K9.
- Next row: P.
- Next row: K.
- Next row: P.
- Repeat last 4 rows four times more. [37 sts]
- Next row: K9, m1, K to last 9 sts, m1, K9.
- Next row: P.
- Repeat last 2 rows nine times more. [57 sts]
- Work 4 rows in st st, beg with a K row.
- Next row: K9, (k2tog) 9 times, K3, (ssk) 9 times, K9. [39 sts]
- Next row: P.

You will need

FOR THE DOLL

30 g (1 oz) of dark brown DK yarn

A small amount of cream DK yarn for the horns

A small amount of black and pale pink DK yarn for the features

20 g (¾ oz) of polyester toy stuffing

EQUIPMENT

A pair of 3 mm (US 2/3) knitting needles

A size 3.25 mm (US D-3) crochet hook

A yarn needle to sew the ox together

- Next row: Cast off 5 sts, K to end.
- Next row: Cast off 5 sts pwise, K to end. [29 sts]
- Work 9 rows in st st, beg with a K row.
- Next row: K.
- Next row: k2 tog, K to last 2 sts, ssk.
- Next row: P.
- Repeat last 2 rows once more. [25 sts]
- Next row: (s1, k2tog, psso) 4 times, K1, (s1, k2tog, psso) 4 times. [9 sts]
- Next row: (p2tog) twice, P1, (p2tog) twice. [5 sts]
- Break yarn, thread it through the remaining sts, pull it up and secure.

Front legs

Make 2 identical pieces.

- Cast on 15 sts in dark brown.
- K 4 rows.
- Work 18 rows in st st, beg with a K row.
- Cast off.

Back legs

Make 2 identical pieces.

- Cast on 15 sts in dark brown.
- K 4 rows.
- Work 22 rows in st st, beg with a K row.
- Cast off.

Ears

Make 2 identical pieces.

- Cast on 5 sts in dark brown.
- K 4 rows.
- Next row: k2tog, K1, k2tog.
- Next row: s1, k2tog, psso.
- Break yarn and pull through remaining st.

Horns

Make 2 identical pieces.

- Cast on 7 sts in cream.
- Cast off 7 sts.

Tail

Use the crochet hook and dark brown yarn, doubled, to crochet a chain (see page 19), 6 cm (2½ in) long. Break the yarn, pull the thread through the last chain and pull tightly. Trim your yarn about 3 cm (1¼ in) away from the end of the chain and fray the yarn ends to represent the switch.

To make up the ox

Join the seams along the lower edge of the head, the front of neck and the underneath of the body. Stuff the ox fairly firmly then sew the back end seam.

   Join the lower and side seams of the legs and stuff firmly. Sew the legs in place on the side of the ox using the photograph as a guide. Oversew the ears and horns in place. Sew the tail in position. If you like, add a few curls of yarn on the ox's forehead.

   Using black yarn, embroider two French knots for the eyes and, using pink yarn, embroider two French knots for the nostrils.

Ass

The ass is knitted in a beautiful flecked grey yarn. The yarn has a natural fuzzy feeling to it that I thought would be just perfect for him. As a finishing touch, I decided to knit a little pink and red blanket for his back.

THE ASS IS APPROXIMATELY 12 CM (4¾ IN) HIGH AND ABOUT 13 CM (5¼ IN) LONG.

Body

The body and head are knitted as one piece.

- Cast on 18 sts in flecked grey.
- Work 12 rows in st st, beg with a K row.
- Next row: K2, k2tog, K to last 4 sts, ssk, K2.
- Next row: P.
- Repeat these 2 rows once more. [14 sts]
  - Next row: K.
  - Mark beg and end of last row with contrasting thread to mark the two ends of the centre back of the body.
  - Next row: P.
  - Next row: K2, m1, K to last 2 sts, m1, K2.
  - Repeat last 2 rows once more. [18 sts]
  - Work 11 rows in st st, beg with a P row.
  - Cast off.

Position your work with the right side facing you.

- **Pick up and K 12 sts along one side of the front end of the body then cast on 34 sts. [46 sts]**
- **Work 9 rows in st st, beg with a P row.**
- **Next row: Cast off 16 sts, K to end.**
- **Next row: Cast off 16 sts pwise, P to end. [14 sts]**
- **Work 5 rows in st st, beg with a K row.**
- **Next row: K.**
- **Work 4 rows st st, beg with a K row.**
- **Next row: K1, (s1, k2tog, psso) 4 times, K1. [6 sts]**
- **Next row: (s1pwise, p2tog, psso) twice.**
- **Next row: k2tog, break yarn and pull through remaining st.**

Legs

Make 4 identical pieces.

- **Cast on 8 sts in flecked grey.**
- **K 4 rows.**
- **Work 16 rows st st, beg with a K row.**
- **Cast off loosely.**

Ears

Make 2 identical pieces.

- **Cast on 4 sts in flecked grey.**
- **K 12 rows.**
- **Next row: (k2tog) twice. [2 sts]**
- **Next row: k2tog, break yarn and pull through remaining st.**

Mane

For the mane, use the crochet hook and dark grey yarn to crochet a chain (see page 19), 35 cm (14 in) long. Gather the mane into a series of evenly spaced loops. Thread a needle on to the tail yarn and pick up one of the individual chain loops every 2 cm (¾ in) along the entire length of the chain. Arrange the loops along the length of yarn so that it is just the right length to run from between the ass's ears to the base of the neck.

Tail

For the tail, use the crochet hook and dark grey yarn to crochet a chain (see page 19), 4 cm (1½ in) long. Trim your yarn about 1 cm (⅜ in) away from the end of the chain and fray the yarn ends to represent the switch.

To make up the ass

Join the seams along the underside of the head and the front of neck. Sew the unattached front side of the body to the unattached side of the neck. Then sew the seam at the back of neck. Sew the seam at the back end. Stuff the ass, then sew the lower body seam.

Join the lower and side seams of the legs and stuff firmly. Sew the legs in place. Pinch the ears in half lengthways and oversew in position. Sew the mane and tail in position.

Embroider the cross-shaped markings on the ass's back (see photograph on page 76) using dark grey yarn and chain stitch (see page 19).

Using black yarn, embroider two French knots for the eyes.

Blanket

- **Cast on 14 sts in pink.**
- **K 2 rows.**
- **Next row: K.**
- **Next row: K2, P to last 2 sts, K2.**
- **Repeat last 2 rows once more.**
- **Join red yarn and K 2 rows.**
- **Break red yarn and continue working in pink yarn.**
- **Next row: K.**
- **Next row: K2, P to last 2 sts, K2.**
- **Repeat last 2 rows 14 times more.**
- **Join red yarn and K 2 rows.**
- **Break red yarn and continue working in pink yarn.**
- **Next row: K.**
- **Next row: K2, P to last 2 sts, K2.**
- **Repeat last 2 rows once more.**
- **K 2 rows.**
- **Cast off.**

A Child is Born

Joseph went out to fetch firewood, feeling very worried. In those days, there were no hospitals and women often died in childbirth. Mary was very young and there was no one around who could help her. Sheep were bleating, oxen were lowing, and asses were braying into the night sky as he built his fire. Joseph began to pray to God that He would keep Mary safe. *"Please watch over her,"* he said, with tears in his eyes.

Suddenly, everything went very quiet and still. The sheep and oxen and asses fell silent. Even the flames of the fire stopped flickering and crackling. Up above, a star as bright as a million suns appeared, lighting up the little stable.

Mary called out: *"Joseph, come in here."* He went inside and the whole room was lit up with a strange and wonderful light. In Mary's arms lay a perfect little baby boy. *"Look,"* she said, holding him out. *"The Son of God is born."*

Joseph kissed her, then he gazed at the beautiful child, whose eyes were wide open and looking straight back at him. Most new babies cry, but this one had a calm, peaceful expression on his face.

"I'll make a bed for him," Joseph said. He found a wooden manger, which the animals' food had been in. He lined it carefully with the softest straw he could find. Mary wrapped the baby tightly in lots of clean white cloths she had brought with her, and they laid him gently in the manger.

Behind them, all the animals in the stable watched, without making a sound. It was as though they knew that something extraordinary had just happened. They knew this was a very special night.

Baby Jesus

Baby Jesus can be posed tucked right into his swaddling cloth, as in a traditional Nativity scene. But if you prefer, why not have his little arms reaching out to his mum and dad? Or, just for fun, see how cute he looks with a little toe poking out. If you think he's getting a bit hot, see how sweet he looks in just his cream knitted underwear.

Doll

Make 2 identical pieces for the front and back.
The body and head are knitted as one piece, starting at the lower edge of the body.

- Cast on 10 sts in beige.
- Next row: K1, inc 1, K to last 2 sts, inc 1, K1.
- Next row: P.
- Next row: K1, m1, K to last st, m1, K1. [14 sts]
- Work 7 rows in st st, beg with a P row.
- Next row: K2, k2tog, K to last 4 sts, ssk, K2.
- Next row: P.
- Next row: K2, k2tog, K to last 4 sts, ssk, K2.
- Next row: p2tog, P to last 2 sts, p2tog.
- Next row: K2, k2tog, ssk, K2. [6 sts]
- Next row: P.
- Next row: K1, m1, K1, m1, K2, m1, K1, m1, K1.
- Next row: P.
- Next row: K1, m1, K1, m1, K to last 2 sts, m1, K1, m1, K1. [14 sts]
- Work 3 rows in st st, beg with a P row.
- Next row: (k2tog) 3 times, K2, (ssk) 3 times.
- Next row: p2 tog, P to last 2 sts, p2tog.
- Next row: K1, k2tog, ssk, K1.
- Next row: (p2tog) twice.
- Next row: k2tog, break yarn and pull through remaining sts.

You will need

FOR THE DOLL

A small amount of light beige DK yarn

A small amount of dark yellow DK yarn for the hair

Small amounts of black and red DK yarn for the features

A small amount of polyester toy stuffing

FOR THE CLOTHES AND SWADDLING CLOTH

A small amount of cream DK yarn

A 10-cm (4-in) length of gold cord for the halo and some gold or invisible thread for sewing it on

EQUIPMENT

A pair of 3 mm (US 2/3) knitting needles

A yarn needle to sew the figure and clothes together

Arms and legs

Make 4 identical pieces (the arms and legs are identical).

- Cast on 5 sts in beige.
- Work 10 rows in st st, beg with a K row.
- Cast off.

To make up, join the two head and body pieces around the head and sides, leaving the lower edge open. Stuff the piece then seam the lower edge. Seam the arms and legs but do not stuff them. Stitch the legs to the lower edge of the body at the outer corners. Stitch the arms to the body, just below the neck.

Using dark yellow yarn, work a few French knots along the top seam of the head for the hair.

Using the black yarn, make two French knots for the eyes.

Untwist a short piece of red yarn into two even strands. Using one of the strands, embroider a 'V' shape for the mouth.

Pants

- Cast on 12 sts in cream.
- K 2 rows.
- Work 5 rows st st, beg with a P row.
- Next row: Cast off 3 sts, K to end.
- Next row: Cast off 3 sts pwise, P to end. [6 sts]
- Work 6 rows in st st, beg with a K row.
- Next row: Cast on 3 sts, K to end.
- Next row: Cast on 3 sts, P to end. [12 sts]
- Work 4 rows in st st beg with a K row.
- K 2 rows.
- Cast off.

To make up, join the side seams.

Swaddling cloth and hood

- Cast on 22 sts in cream.
- K 2 rows.
- Work 2 rows in st st, beg with a K row.
- Next row: K2, m1, (K3, m1) 6 times, K2. [29 sts]

- Next row: P.
- K 3 rows.
- Repeat last 4 rows twice more.
- Next row: P.
- Next row: K.
- Next row: P.
- Next row: (k2tog) 7 times, K1, (k2tog) 7 times. [15 sts]
- Cast off.

Join the back seam.

To make the hood, pick up and K 14 sts across the back of the cloth, from the inside, leaving 8 sts free at the front.

- Next row: K.
- Next row: K1, P to last st, K1.
- Repeat last 2 rows twice more.
- Next row: Cast off 3 sts, K to end.
- Next row: Cast off 3 sts, P to end. [8 sts]
- Work 4 rows in st st, beg with a K row.
- K 2 rows.
- Cast off.

To make up, join the two seams to shape the top part of the hood. The sides of the small square at the end should be seamed around the corner of the main part of the hood to form a hat shape.

Halo

Make a circle from the gold cord, overlapping the ends by 1 cm (⅜ in). Sew on to the back of the head or hood with invisible or gold thread.

Angels Visit the Shepherds

In a field just outside Bethlehem, some shepherds were guarding their sheep in case a bigger animal like a wolf came and attacked them. It was very dark and cold and they huddled together, chatting amongst themselves.

Suddenly there appeared a light so bright that it hurt their eyes. They squinted to see where the light was coming from and were terrified when they made out the form of a huge angel. It appeared to be standing on a cloud just above them. *"Help!"* they yelled in fear. *"Don't hurt us!"*

"Don't be afraid," the angel said, in a voice that was neither a man's nor a woman's, but a musical sound that was pure and beautiful. *"I bring you news of great joy for all the people on earth."*

The shepherds looked round at each other. Each one thought at first that he must have fallen asleep and that this was all part of a dream – until he realized that all the other shepherds were having the same dream. The angel was such a brilliant white colour that it was difficult to look at directly.

The angel continued: *"Today in Bethlehem a baby has been born. He is the one that will save the world. You will know this baby because he will be wrapped in white cloths and lying in a manger."*

As the shepherds watched, the whole night sky was filled with more angels, singing *"Glory to God, and peace to all people on earth"*. It was the most wonderful sight they had ever seen. Gradually the angels floated out of sight, leaving the shepherds in the field staring after them with their mouths hanging open.

"We must go and find this child," one of the shepherds said.

"Yes, we must," they all agreed.

You will need

FOR THE DOLL

20 g (¾ oz) of dark beige DK yarn

Small amounts of black and red DK yarn for the features

A small amount of dark brown DK yarn for the hair

15 g (½ oz) of polyester toy stuffing

FOR THE CLOTHES AND WINGS

20 g (¾ oz) of white DK yarn

A small amount of dark yellow yarn

A small amount of pale green DK yarn for the wings

A small amount of purple DK yarn for the hair band

A small white heart-shaped button and some bright green thread for the dress

EQUIPMENT

A pair of 3 mm (US 2/3) knitting needles

A size 3.25 mm (US D-3) crochet hook

A yarn needle to sew the figure and clothes together

Angel

I've chosen a classic white woollen yarn for my angel's robe and a demure pale green for the wings. If you've stumbled across something with a bit of texture or sparkle, you might want to dress him in something a little more outrageous. The same doll, or a similar version of it, can be used both for the angel who appears before the shepherds and for Angel Gabriel.

Doll

Using the dark beige yarn, knit, make up and stuff the basic figure as described on pages 20–1.

Using the black yarn, make two French knots for the eyes.

Untwist a short piece of red yarn into two even strands. Using one of the strands, embroider a 'V' shape for the mouth.

For the hair, use the crochet hook and dark brown yarn to crochet two chains (see page 19), each 35 cm (14 in) long. Arrange the first chain in four even-sized loops and secure these to one side of the head. Do the same with the second cord, securing it to the other side of the head.

Dress

Make 2 identical pieces for the front and back. The dress pieces are knitted from the bottom to the top (neck) edge.

- Cast on 22 sts in white.
- K 4 rows.
- Join dark yellow yarn and work 2 rows in st st, beg with a K row.
- Break yarn and continue working in white yarn.
- Work 2 rows st st, beg with a K row.
- Next row: K2, k2tog, K to last 4 sts, ssk, K2.
- Next row: P.
- Repeat last 2 rows three times more. [14 sts]
- Work 16 rows in st st, beg with a K row.
- Mark beg and end of last row with a piece of contrasting yarn or thread.
- Work 5 rows in st st, beg with a K row.
- K 3 rows.
- Cast off loosely.

Seam the dress pieces together 2 sts along at each side of the neck opening and join the shoulder seams.

For the sleeves, spread the two dress pieces apart. With the right side of your work facing you, pick up and K 14 sts between the two thread markers on one side of the dress.

- Work 9 rows in st st, beg with a P row.
- Next row: K2, m1, K to last 2 sts, m1, K2.
- Next row: P.
- Repeat last 2 rows three times more. [22 sts]
- Cast off loosely.

Complete the second sleeve in exactly the same way. Remove the thread markers.

To make up, join the underarm and side seams. Sew the button in place using bright green thread.

Wings

Make 2 identical pieces.

- Cast on 8 sts in pale green.
- K 2 rows.
- Next row: K2, (m1, K2) 3 times. [11 sts]
- Work 3 rows st st, beg with a P row.
- Next row: (K2, m1) 5 times, K1. [16 sts]
- Next row: P.
- Next row: K2, (yfwd, k2tog) 6 times, K2.
- Next row: P.
- K 2 rows.
- Cast off loosely.

Sew the wings to the back of the doll once the dress is in place. The right side of the wings should face the back of the doll so that you see the wings' right side when you look at the doll from the front.

Hairband

For the hairband, use the crochet hook and purple yarn to crochet a chain (see page 19), 19 cm (7½ in) long.

Wrap the hairband around the angel's head and tie in a knot.

The Shepherds Visit the Stable

The shepherds rushed down to Bethlehem straight away to find the special child. They couldn't stop talking about what had just happened to them.

A young shepherd asked, *"Do you think we are the only people who know, or have the angels told anyone else?"* They had no idea.

"Where do you think this stable will be?" another one wondered.

"I know exactly where the stable is," said an old shepherd.

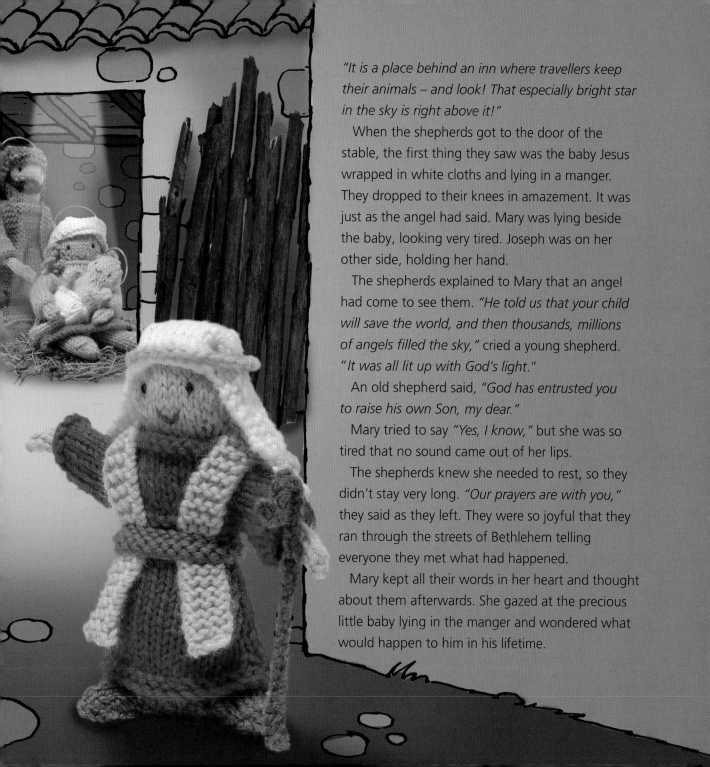

"It is a place behind an inn where travellers keep their animals – and look! That especially bright star in the sky is right above it!"

When the shepherds got to the door of the stable, the first thing they saw was the baby Jesus wrapped in white cloths and lying in a manger. They dropped to their knees in amazement. It was just as the angel had said. Mary was lying beside the baby, looking very tired. Joseph was on her other side, holding her hand.

The shepherds explained to Mary that an angel had come to see them. *"He told us that your child will save the world, and then thousands, millions of angels filled the sky,"* cried a young shepherd. *"It was all lit up with God's light."*

An old shepherd said, *"God has entrusted you to raise his own Son, my dear."*

Mary tried to say *"Yes, I know,"* but she was so tired that no sound came out of her lips.

The shepherds knew she needed to rest, so they didn't stay very long. *"Our prayers are with you,"* they said as they left. They were so joyful that they ran through the streets of Bethlehem telling everyone they met what had happened.

Mary kept all their words in her heart and thought about them afterwards. She gazed at the precious little baby lying in the manger and wondered what would happen to him in his lifetime.

You will need

FOR THE DOLL

20 g (¾ oz) of dark beige DK yarn

Small amounts of black and red DK yarn
for the features

A small amount of grey DK yarn for the beard

A small amount of dark brown DK yarn
for the sandals

15 g (½ oz) of polyester toy stuffing

FOR THE CLOTHES AND ACCESSORIES

20 g (¾ oz) of mustard DK yarn

A small amount of pale yellow DK yarn

A small amount of dark brown DK yarn

10 g (¼–½ oz) of cream DK yarn

A small amount of mid-blue DK yarn

A 13-cm (5¼-in) length of PVC-covered
garden wire for the crook

EQUIPMENT

A pair of 3 mm (US 2/3) knitting needles

A pair of 2.25 mm (US 1) knitting needles
(for the beard only)

A size 3.25 mm (US D-3) crochet hook

A yarn needle to sew the figure
and clothes together

Shepherds

Trusty and hardworking, these shepherds are a Knitivity essential. I chose muted tones and natural yarns for their clothes, mainly because I thought this was what shepherds probably wore. Their crooks are made from a really thin knitted strip which I sewed over some wire. This is much easier to do than you'd think.

FIRST SHEPHERD

Doll

Using the dark beige yarn, knit, make up and stuff the basic figure as described on pages 20–1.

Using the black yarn, make two French knots for the eyes.

Untwist a short piece of red yarn into two even strands. Using one of the strands, embroider a 'V' shape for the mouth.

To make the shepherd's toe-post sandals, sew a large 'V' shape on the top of each foot using dark brown yarn.

Beard

The beard is knitted from the part of the beard on the chin to the pointed end.

- **Using 2.25 mm (US 1) needles, cast on 7 sts in grey, leaving a long tail for making one of the sideburns.**
- **K 5 rows.**
- **Next row: k2tog, K3, ssk.**
- **Next row: K.**
- **Next row: k2tog, K1, ssk.**
- **Next row: s1, k2tog, psso.**
- **Break the yarn leaving a long tail, then pull through remaining st.**

Using the crochet hook, crochet a 2-cm (¾-in) chain (see page 19) with the starting tail of yarn.

Thread the tail at the tip of the beard up through the side of the beard to the top and make a matching chain for the second sideburn. Sew the beard in place around the face, using the photograph as a guide.

Tunic

Make 2 identical pieces for the front and back. The tunic pieces are knitted from the bottom to the top (neck) edge.

- **Cast on 22 sts in mustard.**
- **K 4 rows.**
- **Work 4 rows in st st, beg with a K row.**
- **Join pale yellow yarn.**

- **K 2 rows.**
- **Break yarn and continue working in mustard.**
- **Work 2 rows in st st, beg with a K row.**
- **Next row: K2, k2tog, K to last 4 sts, ssk, K2.**
- **Next row: P.**
- **Next row: K.**
- **Next row: P.**
- **Repeat last 4 rows twice more. [16 sts]**
- **Work 8 rows in st st, beg with a K row.**
- **K 2 rows.**
- **Work 8 rows in st st, beg with a K row.**
- **Next row: Cast off 2 sts, K to end.**
- **Repeat last row once more. [12 sts]**
- **Cast off.**

Seam the tunic pieces together 2 sts along at each side of the neck opening to form the shoulder seams.

For the sleeves, spread the two tunic pieces apart. With the right side of your work facing you, pick up and K 16 sts between the two rows of mustard garter stitch.

- **Work 15 rows in st st, beg with a P row.**
- **K4 rows.**
- **Cast off loosely.**

Complete the second sleeve in exactly the same way as the first sleeve.

To make up, join the underarm and side seams.

Scarf

- **Cast on 5 sts in pale yellow.**
- **Work in garter stitch until the scarf measures 23 cm (9 in).**
- **Cast off.**

Belt

- **Cast on 28 sts in dark brown.**
- **K 2 rows.**
- **Cast off.**

Fasten around the shepherd and his scarf and sew the short sides together at the back.

Headddress

The headdress is knitted from the top to the bottom.

- Cast on 10 sts in cream.
- K 2 rows.
- Work 6 rows in st st beg with a K row.
- Next row: Cast on 4 sts, K to end of row.
- Next row: Cast on 4 sts, P to end. [18 sts]
- Next row: K.
- Next row: P.
- Next row: K.
- Next row: K2, P to last 2 sts, K2.
- Repeat last 2 rows three times more.
- Next row: K2, (m1, K2) 8 times. [26 sts]
- Next row: K2, P to last 2 sts, K2.
- Next row: K2, m1, K to last 2 sts, m1, K2.
- Next row: K2, P to last 2 sts, K2.
- Repeat last 2 rows three times more. [34 sts]
- Join blue yarn and K 2 rows.
- Break yarn and continue working in cream.
- Next row: K.
- Next row: K2, P to last 2 sts, K2.
- K 2 rows.
- Cast off loosely.

To make up, join the two seams to shape the top part of the headdress. The sides of the small square at the beginning should be seamed around the corner of the main part of the headdress to form a hat shape.

For the headdress cord, use the crochet hook and mid-blue yarn to crochet a chain (see page 19), 11 cm (4½ in) long. Slip stitch the ends of the chain together to form a circle. Weave loose ends through the chain and trim.

Crook

- Cast on 40 sts in dark brown.
- K 1 row.
- Cast off.

Sew the knitted strip around the length of wire and bend the top to shape the crook handle.

You will need

FOR THE DOLL

20 g (¾ oz) of light beige DK yarn

Small amounts of black and red DK yarn for the features

A small amount of brown DK yarn for the beard

A small amount of dark brown DK yarn for the sandals

15 g (½ oz) of polyester toy stuffing

FOR THE CLOTHES AND ACCESSORIES

20 g (¾ oz) of pale green DK yarn

A small amount of olive green DK yarn

A small amount of dark brown DK yarn

10 g (¼–½ oz) of cream DK yarn

A small amount of red DK yarn

A small amount of dark grey DK yarn

A 13-cm (5¼-in) length of PVC-covered garden wire for the crook

EQUIPMENT

A pair of 3 mm (US 2/3) knitting needles

A pair of 2.25 mm (US 1) knitting needles (for the beard only)

A size 3.25 mm (US D-3) crochet hook

A yarn needle to sew the figure and clothes together

SECOND SHEPHERD
Doll

Using the light beige yarn, knit, make up and stuff the basic figure as described on pages 20–1.

Using the black yarn, make two French knots for the eyes.

Untwist a short piece of red yarn into two even strands. Using one of the strands, embroider a 'V' shape for the mouth.

To make the shepherd's sandals, sew a large cross stitch on the top of each foot using dark brown yarn.

Beard

The beard is knitted from the part of the beard on the chin to the pointed end.

- Using 2.25 mm (US 1) needles, cast on 7 sts in brown, leaving a long tail for making one of the sideburns.
- K 5 rows.
- Next row: k2tog, K3, ssk.
- Next row: K.
- Next row: k2tog, K1, ssk.
- Next row: s1, k2tog, psso.
- Break the yarn leaving a long tail, then pull through remaining st.

Using the crochet hook, crochet a 2-cm (¾-in) chain (see page 19) with the starting tail of yarn.

Thread the tail at the tip of the beard up through the side of the beard to the top and make a matching chain for the second sideburn. Sew the beard in place around the face, using the photograph as a guide.

Tunic

Make 2 identical pieces for the front and back. The tunic pieces are knitted from the bottom to the top (neck) edge.

- Cast on 22 sts in pale green.
- K 4 rows.
- Work 4 rows in st st, beg with a K row.
- Join olive green yarn.
- K 2 rows.
- Break yarn and continue working in pale green.
- Work 2 rows in st st, beg with a K row.
- Next row: K2, k2tog, K to last 4 sts, ssk, K2.
- Next row: P.
- Next row: K.
- Next row: P.
- Repeat last 4 rows twice more. [16 sts]
- Work 8 rows in st st, beg with a K row.
- K 2 rows.
- Work 8 rows in st st, beg with a K row.

- **Next row: Cast off 2 sts, K to end.**
- **Repeat last row once more. [12 sts]**
- **Cast off.**

Seam the tunic pieces together 2 sts along at each side of the neck opening to form the shoulder seams.

For the sleeves, spread the two tunic pieces apart. With the right side of your work facing you, pick up and K 16 sts between the two rows of pale green garter stitch.

- **Work 15 rows in st st, beg with a P row.**
- **K 4 rows.**
- **Cast off loosely.**

Complete the second sleeve in exactly the same way as the first sleeve.

To make up, join the underarm and side seams.

Scarf

- **Cast on 5 sts in olive green.**
- **Work in garter stitch until the scarf measures 23 cm (9 in).**
- **Cast off.**

Belt

- **Cast on 28 sts in dark brown.**
- **K 2 rows.**
- **Cast off.**

Fasten around the shepherd and his scarf and sew the short sides together at the back.

Headdress

The headdress is knitted from the top to the bottom.

- **Cast on 10 sts in cream.**
- **K 2 rows.**
- **Work 6 rows in st st, beg with a K row.**
- **Next row: Cast on 4 sts, K to end.**
- **Next row: Cast on 4 sts, P to end. [18 sts]**
- **Next row: K.**
- **Next row: P.**
- **Next row: K.**
- **Next row: K2, P to last 2 sts, K2.**
- **Repeat last 2 rows three times more.**
- **Next row: K2, (m1, K2) 8 times. [26 sts]**
- **Next row: K2, P to last 2 sts, K2.**
- **Next row: K2, m1, K to last 2 sts, m1, K2.**
- **Next row: K2, P to last 2 sts, K2.**
- **Repeat last 2 rows three times more. [34 sts]**
- **Join red yarn and K 2 rows.**
- **Break yarn and continue working in cream.**
- **Next row: K.**
- **Next row: K2, P to last 2 sts, K2.**
- **K 2 rows.**
- **Cast off loosely.**

To make up, join the two seams to shape the top part of the headdress. The sides of the small square at the beginning should be seamed around the corner of the main part of the headdress to form a hat shape.

For the headdress cord, use the crochet hook and red yarn to crochet a chain (see page 19), 11 cm (4½ in) long. Slip stitch the ends of the chain together to form a circle. Weave loose ends through the chain and trim.

Crook

- **Cast on 40 sts in dark grey.**
- **K 1 row.**
- **Cast off.**

Sew the knitted strip around the length of wire and bend the top to shape the crook handle.

You will need

FOR THE DOLL

15 g (½ oz) of light beige DK yarn

10 g (¼–½ oz) of olive green DK yarn
for the boots

Small amounts of black and red DK yarn
for the features

10 g (¼–½ oz) of polyester toy stuffing

FOR THE CLOTHES AND ACCESSORIES

15 g (½ oz) of red DK yarn

A small amount of pink DK yarn

A small amount of mid-blue DK yarn

10 g (¼–½ oz) of cream DK yarn

A small amount of light green DK yarn

A small amount of dark grey DK yarn

A 10-cm (4-in) length of PVC-covered
garden wire for the crook

EQUIPMENT

A pair of 3 mm (US 2/3) knitting needles

A size 3.25 mm (US D-3) crochet hook

A yarn needle to sew the figure and
clothes together

SHEPHERD BOY
Doll

The shepherd boy is knitted in a similar way to the Basic Standing Doll (see pages 20–1), but is shorter.

Front

The front is worked as one piece, from the tip of the feet to the top of the head.

- Cast on 5 sts in olive green for the first boot.
- Work 6 rows in st st, beg with a K row.
- Break yarn and leave sts on the needle.
- On the same needle, cast on 5 sts for the second boot.
- Work 6 rows in st st on these sts only, beg with a K row.

- Next row: K5 sts across second boot, cast on 5 sts, K5 sts across first boot. [15 sts]
- Next row: P.
- ** Work 8 rows in st st, beg with a K row.
- Next row: K1, k2tog, K to last 3 sts, ssk, K1. [13 sts]
- Next row: P
- Break yarn and join light beige yarn.
- Work 6 rows in st st, beg with a K row.
- Next row: K1, k2tog, K to last 3 sts, ssk, K1. [11 sts]
- Work 13 rows in st st, beg with a P row.
- Next row: K1, k2tog, K to last 3 sts, ssk, K1. [9 sts]
- Next row: P.
- Next row: K2, m1, K1, m1, K3, m1, K1, m1, K2.
- Next row: P.
- Repeat last 2 rows once more. [17 sts]
- Next row: K2, m1, K to last 2 sts, m1, K2. [19 sts]
- Next row: P.
- Next row: k2tog, K2, (k2tog) twice, K3, (ssk) twice, K2, ssk. [13 sts]
- Next row: p2tog, P to last 2 sts, p2tog. [11 sts]
- Next row: (k2tog) twice, K3, (ssk) twice. [7 sts]
- Next row: p2tog, P to last 2 sts, p2tog.
- Cast off remaining 5 sts firmly.

Back

The back of the doll is worked as one piece, from the base to the top of the head.

- Cast on 15 sts in olive green.
- Work 2 rows in st st, beg with a K row.
- Work as for the doll front from ** to end.

Base

- Cast on 5 sts in olive green for the first boot.
- Work 6 rows in st st, beg with a K row.
- Break yarn and leave sts on the needle.
- On the same needle, cast on 5 sts for the second boot.
- Work 6 rows in st st on these sts only, beg with a K row.
- Next row: K5 sts across second boot, cast on 3 sts, K5 sts across first boot. [13 sts]
- Work 5 rows in st st, beg with a P row.
- Next row: k2tog, K to last 2 sts, ssk.
- Next row: P.
- Repeat last 2 rows once more. [9 sts]
- Next row: k2tog, K to last 2 sts, ssk.
- Next row: p2tog, P to last 2 sts, p2tog. [5 sts]
- Cast off.

Arms

Make 2 identical pieces. Each arm is knitted as one piece from the top of the arm to the tip of the hand.

- Cast on 7 sts in light beige.
- Work 16 rows in st st, beg with a K row.
- Next row: K1, k2tog, K1, ssk, K1. [5 sts]
- Cast off purlwise.

Make up and stuff the doll as described on pages 20–1.

Using the black yarn, make two French knots for the eyes.

Untwist a short piece of red yarn into two even strands. Using one of the strands, embroider a 'V' shape for the mouth.

Tunic

Make 2 identical pieces for the front and back. The tunic pieces are knitted from the bottom to the top (neck) edge.

- Cast on 20 sts in red.
- K 2 rows.
- Work 2 rows in st st, beg with a K row.

- Next row: K2, k2tog, K to last 4 sts, ssk, K2.
- Next row: P.
- Next row: K.
- Next row: P.
- Rep last 4 rows twice more. [14 sts]
- Work 4 rows in st st, beg with a K row.
- K 2 rows.
- Work 8 rows in st st, beg with a K row.
- Next row: Cast off 2 sts, K to end.
- Repeat last row once more. [10 sts]
- Cast off.

Seam the tunic pieces together 2 sts along at each side of the neck opening to form the shoulder seams.

For the sleeves, spread the two tunic pieces apart. With the right side of your work facing you, pick up and K 16 sts between the two rows of red garter stitch.
- Work 9 rows in st st, beg with a P row.
- K 2 rows.
- Cast off loosely.

Complete the second sleeve in exactly the same way as the first sleeve.

To make up, join the underarm and side seams.

Scarf

- Cast on 4 sts in pink.
- Work in garter stitch until the scarf measures 19 cm (7½ in).
- Cast off.

Belt

- Cast on 26 sts in mid-blue.
- K 2 rows.
- Cast off.

Fasten around the shepherd boy and his scarf and sew the short sides together at the back.

Headdress

The headdress is knitted from the top to the bottom.
- Cast on 10 sts in cream.
- K 2 rows.
- Work 6 rows in st st, beg with a K row.
- Next row: Cast on 4 sts, K to end.
- Next row: Cast on 4 sts, P to end. [18 sts]
- Next row: K.
- Next row: P.
- Next row: K.
- Next row: K2, P to last 2 sts, K2.
- Repeat last 2 rows three times more.
- Next row: K2, (m1, K2) 8 times. [26 sts]
- Next row: K2, P to last 2 sts, K2.
- Next row: K2, m1, K to last 2 sts, m1, K2.
- Next row: K2, P to last 2 sts, K2.
- Repeat last 2 rows once more. [30 sts]
- Join light green yarn and K 2 rows.
- Break yarn and continue working in cream.
- Next row: K.
- Next row: K2, P to last 2 sts, K2.
- K 2 rows.
- Cast off loosely.

To make up, join the two seams to shape the top part of the headdress. The sides of the small square at the beginning should be seamed round the corner of the main part of the headdress to form a hat shape.

For the headdress cord, use the crochet hook and pale green yarn to crochet a chain (see page 19), 11 cm (4½ in) long. Slip stitch ends of the chain together to form a circle. Weave loose ends through the chain and trim.

Crook

- Cast on 32 sts in dark grey.
- K 1 row.
- Cast off.

Sew the knitted strip around the length of wire and bend the top to shape the crook handle.

Sheep

I've knitted the sheep's coats in some textured yarns that I found in my local knitting store but you could use a regular cream yarn if you prefer. If you want to use a textured yarn, make sure you choose one that is roughly equivalent to DK yarn so that it will be easy to knit on your regular needles.

There are two sizes of sheep. The larger one is lying down so you do not need to knit the legs. The smaller sheep has legs.

THE LARGE SHEEP IS APPROXIMATELY 4 CM (1½ IN) HIGH AND 10 CM (4 IN) LONG. THE SMALL SHEEP IS APPROXIMATELY 5 CM (2 IN) HIGH AND 8 CM (3¼ IN) LONG.

LARGE SHEEP (LYING DOWN)
Body and head

- Cast on 24 sts in cream.
- Work 24 rows in st st, beg with a K row.
- Next row: Cast off 5 sts, K to end.
- Next row: Cast off 5 sts pwise, P to end and break yarn. [14 sts]
- Next row: Join beige yarn and K to end.
- Work 5 rows in st st, beg with a P row.
- Next row: K1, (s1, k2tog, psso) 4 times, K1. [6 sts]
- Break yarn, thread it through the remaining sts, pull it up and secure.

Ears

Make 2 identical pieces.

- Using 2.25 mm (US 1) needles, cast on 3 sts in beige.
- K 4 rows.
- Next row: s1, k2tog, psso.
- Break yarn and pull through remaining st.

Tail

- Cast on 7 sts in cream.
- Cast off 7 sts.

To make up the large sheep

To make up, seam along the chin, front and lower edge of the sheep, leaving the tail end open for stuffing. Stuff and then close the tail end. Sew the ears and tail in place. Embroider two French knots for the eyes and a small 'Y' shape for the nose and mouth in black yarn, using the photograph as a guide.

You will need

FOR THE DOLL

10 g (¼–½ oz) of specialist cream yarn that is the equivalent of DK yarn

A small amount of yarn for the face and legs

A small amount of black yarn for the features

10 g (¼–½ oz) of polyester toy stuffing

EQUIPMENT

A pair of 3 mm (US 2/3) knitting needles

A pair of 2.25 mm (US 1) knitting needles (for the ears only)

A yarn needle to sew the sheep together

SMALL SHEEP
Body and head

- Cast on 22 sts in cream.
- Work 20 rows in st st, beg with a K row.
- Next row: Cast off 4 sts, K to end.
- Next row: Cast off 4 sts pwise, P to end and break yarn. [14 sts]
- Next row: Join the yarn for the face and K to end.
- Work 5 rows in st st, beg with a P row.
- Next row: K1, (s1, k2tog, psso) 4 times, K1. [6 sts]
- Break yarn, thread it through the remaining sts, pull it up and secure.

Ears

Make 2 identical pieces.

- Using 2.25 mm (US 1) needles, cast on 3 sts in the yarn used for the face.
- K 4 rows.
- Next row: s1, k2tog, psso.
- Break yarn and pull through remaining st.

Tail

- Cast on 7 sts in cream.
- Cast off 7 sts.

Legs

Make 4 identical pieces.

- Cast on 5 sts in the yarn used for the face.
- K 4 rows.
- Cast off.

To make up the small sheep

Seam along the chin, front and lower edge of the sheep, leaving the tail end open for stuffing. Stuff and then close the tail end. Sew the ears and tail in place. Sew the legs into small tubes so that the rows of garter stitch run along the length of the leg. Sew the legs onto the body. Embroider two French knots for the eyes and a small 'Y' shape for the nose and mouth in black yarn.

Following the Star

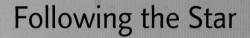

ar away from Bethlehem, in eastern lands, there lived three wise men called Caspar, Melchior and Balthasar. They knew all about the stars, and so they were astonished one night when a new kind of star appeared in the sky. It was brighter than fire, with long white beams that shot outwards and lit up the darkness. Nothing like it had ever been seen before in their lifetimes.

"What does it mean?" Caspar asked.

They took out all their learned scrolls and studied them until they found the answer. It had been prophesied long ago. A star like that meant that a child had been born who would become a very special king. This newborn child would one day save the world.

"We must go and find him so that we can worship him," said Balthasar.

They loaded their camels with food and water for the journey and rolled up special mats that they could sleep on. They put turbans on their heads and wrapped long colourful robes around their bodies to protect themselves when the desert sands blew in the wind. Before they left home, they also chose special gifts to take to the new baby.

"How will we find him?" asked Caspar as they climbed on to their camels.

"Simple!" said Melchior. "We will follow the star."

They looked up at where it twinkled in the sky, almost as though it was winking at them. Then they set off across the desert, sleeping by day and travelling by night in the light of the incredible star. And as they followed it, every night it seemed to get brighter and brighter.

Wise men

If you've got a lot of clashing colours in your knitting stash and have been wondering when they'll come in handy, here's the answer. I've used all sorts of colours for this motley crew, including quite a lot of gold crochet thread to give these wise men something of a regal air. So rifle through your yarns, see what goes with what and get knitting.

FIRST WISE MAN

Doll

Using the mid-brown yarn, knit, make up and stuff the basic figure as described on pages 20–1.

Using the black yarn, make two French knots for the eyes.

Untwist a short piece of red yarn into two even strands. Using one of the strands, embroider a 'V' shape for the mouth.

For the hair, use the crochet hook and black yarn to crochet a chain (see page 19), 13 cm (5¼ in) long. Fold the chain in half and sew it along the head seam, from the middle of the head on one side to the middle of the head on the other side.

To make the sandals, sew two large straight stitches across the top of each foot using gold crochet thread.

Robe

Make 2 identical pieces for the front and back. The robe pieces are knitted from the bottom to the top (neck) edge.

- Cast on 22 sts in orange.
- K 4 rows.
- Break yarn and join yellow yarn.
- Work 8 rows in st st, beg with a K row.
- Next row: K2, k2tog, K to last 4 sts, ssk, K2.
- Next row: P.
- Next row: K.
- Next row: P.
- Repeat last 4 rows twice more. [16 sts]
- Work 8 rows in st st, beg with a K row.
- Mark beg and end of last row with a piece of contrasting yarn or thread.
- Work 10 rows in st st, beg with a K row.
- Next row: Cast off 2 sts, K to end.
- Repeat last row once more. [12 sts]
- Cast off.

Seam the robe pieces together 2 sts along at each side of the neck opening to form the shoulder seams.

For the sleeves, spread the two robe pieces apart. With the right side of your work facing you, pick up and K 16 sts between the two thread markers.

- Work 11 rows in st st, beg with a P row.
- Next row: K2, m1, K to last 2 sts, m1, K2.
- Next row: P.
- Repeat last 2 rows twice more. [22 sts]
- Break yarn and join orange yarn.
- K 2 rows.
- Cast off loosely.

Complete the second sleeve in exactly the same way. Remove thread markers.

To make up, join the underarm and side seams.

Belt

Use the crochet hook and two strands of the gold crochet thread to crochet a chain (see page 19), 35 cm (14 in) long. Sew the tails of the chain back through the chain. Wrap the belt twice around the wise man's waist and secure in a loose knot.

Cape

The cape is knitted in one piece, from the neck edge to the lower edge.

- Cast on 24 sts in green, leaving a long tail of yarn for making the button loop.
- K 2 rows.
- Next row: K5, inc 1 into next 2 sts, K10, inc 1 into next 2 sts, K5.
- Next and every ws row: K2, P to last 2 sts, K2.
- Next rs row: K6, inc 1 into next 2 sts, K12, inc 1 into next 2 sts, K6.
- Next rs row: K7, inc 1 into next 2 sts, K14, inc 1 into next 2 sts, K7.
- Next rs row: K8, inc 1 into next 2 sts, K16, inc 1 into next 2 sts, K8.
- Next rs row: K9, inc 1 into next 2 sts, K18, inc 1 into next 2 sts, K9. [44 sts]
- Next row: K2, P to last 2 sts, K2.

- Next row: K.
- Next row: K2, P to last 2 sts, K2.
- Repeat last 2 rows once more.
- K 2 rows.
- Cast off loosely.

To make up, use the tail at the neck edge and the crochet hook to work a 1-cm (⅜-in) chain for the button loop. Sew the button on to the opposite side of the cape.

Hat

- Cast on 30 sts in gold crochet thread.
- K 2 rows.
- Break yarn and join turquoise yarn.
- Work 4 rows in st st, beg with a K row.
- Next row: Cast off 10 sts, K to end.
- Next row: Cast off 10 sts pwise, P to end. [10 sts]
- Work 6 rows in st st, beg with a K row.
- Cast off.

To make up, sew the back seam to form a circle, then seam the top square of the hat to the top of the circle to form the hat shape.

SECOND WISE MAN
Doll

Using the dark beige yarn, knit, make up and stuff the basic figure as described on pages 20–1.

Using the black yarn, make two French knots for eyes.

Untwist a short piece of red yarn into two even strands. Using one of the strands, embroider a 'V' shape for the mouth.

To make the sandals, sew a large cross stitch on the top of each foot using deep pink yarn.

Beard

The beard is knitted from the part of the beard on the chin to the pointed end.

- **Using 2.25 mm (US 1) needles, cast on 7 sts in mid-brown, leaving a long tail for making one of the sideburns.**
- **K 5 rows.**
- **Next row: k2tog, K3, ssk.**
- **Next row: K.**
- **Next row: k2tog, K1, ssk.**
- **Next row: s1, k2tog, psso.**
- **Break yarn leaving a long tail, pull through remaining st.**

Using the crochet hook, crochet a 2-cm (¾-in) chain (see page 19) with the starting tail of yarn.

Thread the tail at the tip of the beard up through the side of the beard to the top and make a matching chain for the second sideburn. Sew the beard in place around the face, using the photograph as a guide.

Robe

Make 2 identical pieces front and back. The pieces are knitted from the bottom to the top edge.

- **Cast on 22 sts in gold crochet thread.**
- **K 4 rows.**
- **Break yarn and join aqua yarn.**
- **Work 8 rows in st st, beg with a K row.**
- **Next row: K2, k2tog, K to last 4 sts, ssk, K2.**
- **Next row: P.**
- **Next row: K.**
- **Next row: P.**
- **Repeat last 4 rows twice more. [16 sts]**
- **Work 8 rows in st st, beg with a K row.**
- **Mark beg and end of last row with a piece of contrasting yarn or thread.**
- **Work 10 rows in st st, beg with a K row.**
- **Next row: Cast off 2 sts, K to end.**
- **Repeat last row once more. [12 sts]**
- **Cast off.**

Seam the robe pieces together 2 sts along at each side of the neck opening to form the shoulder seams.

For the sleeves, spread the two robe pieces apart. With the right side of your work facing you, pick up and K 16 sts between the two thread markers.

- Work 11 rows in st st, beg with a P row.
- Next row: K2, m1, K to last 2 sts, m1, K2.
- Next row: P.
- Repeat last 2 rows twice more. [22 sts]
- Break yarn and join gold crochet thread.
- K 2 rows.
- Cast off loosely.

Complete the second sleeve in exactly the same way. Remove the thread markers.

To make up, join the underarm and side seams.

Belt

Use the crochet hook and mid-blue yarn to crochet a chain (see page 19), 35 cm (14 in) long. Sew the tails of the chain back through the chain. Wrap the belt twice around the wise man's waist and secure in a loose knot.

Waistcoat

The waistcoat is worked as one piece from the lower edge of the back to the lower edges of the two front sides.

- Cast on 18 sts in pale green.
- K 10 rows.
- Next row: K2, k2tog, K to last 4 sts, ssk, K2.
- K 9 rows.
- Repeat last 10 rows once more. [14 sts]
- Next row: K2, k2tog, K to last 4 sts, ssk, K2. [12 sts]
- K 3 rows.
- Next row: K4, cast off 4 sts, K4 (including st on needle after cast-off).
- Work on the last 4 sts only and leave the other stitches on a safety pin.
- K 3 rows.

- Next row: K2, m1, K2.
- K 9 rows.
- Next row: K to last 2 sts, m1, K2.
- K 9 rows.
- Repeat last 10 rows once more. [7 sts]
- Cast off.

With the wrong side of your work facing you, transfer the sts on the safety pin to one of your knitting needles.

- Starting at the neck edge of the sts, K 3 rows.
- Next row: K2, m1, K2.
- K 9 rows.
- Next row: K2, m1, K to end.
- K 9 rows.
- Repeat last 10 rows once more. [7 sts]
- Cast off.

To make up, join the side seams of the waistcoat, leaving an opening at the top for the armholes.

Turban

- Cast on 38 sts in deep pink.
- K 2 rows.
- Next row: k2tog, K to last 2 sts, ssk.
- Next row: P.
- Repeat last 2 rows twice more. [32 sts]
- Next row: Cast off 4 sts, K to end.
- Next row: Cast off 12 sts pwise, P to end. [16 sts]
- Next row: k2tog, K to last 2 sts, k2tog.
- Next row: p2tog, P to last 2 sts, p2tog.
- Repeat last 2 rows twice more. [4 sts]
- Next row: (k2tog) twice.
- Next row: p2tog.
- Break yarn and pull through remaining st.

To make up, fold the sides inwards to make a turban shape and seam in place. Sew a sequin and a bead to the front of the turban.

THIRD WISE MAN
Doll

The third wise man is worked very similarly to the Basic Standing Doll (see pages 20–1), except the purple shoes are knitted as an integral part of the doll.

Front

- Cast on 2 sts in purple.
- Next row: inc 1, P to end.
- Next row: inc 1, K to end.
- Next row: inc 1, P to end. [5 sts]
- Work 8 rows in st st, beg with a K row.
- Break yarn and leave these sts on the needle.
- Cast on 2 sts on the same needle and knit the second shoe in exactly the same way.
- Break yarn and join beige yarn. Continue working as for the front of the Basic Standing Doll in the normal way, starting at * on the pattern on page 20. Work the back of the doll in the normal way.

Base

- Cast on 2 sts in purple.
- Next row: inc 1, P to end.
- Next row: inc 1, K to end.
- Next row: inc 1, P to end. [5 sts]
- Work 8 rows in st st, beg with a K row.
- Break yarn and leave these sts on the needle.
- Cast on 2 sts on the same needle and knit the second foot in exactly the same way.
- Break yarn and join beige yarn. Continue working as for the base of the Basic Standing Doll in the normal way, starting from * on the pattern on page 21.

Make up and stuff the doll as described on page 21.

Using the black yarn, make two French knots for the eyes.

Untwist a short piece of red yarn into two even strands. Using one of the strands, embroider a 'V' shape for the mouth.

Beard

The beard is knitted from the part of the beard on the chin to the pointed end.

- Using 2.25 mm (US 1) needles, cast on 7 sts in dark brown, leaving a long tail for making one of the sideburns.
- K 5 rows.
- Next row: k2tog, K3, ssk.
- Next row: K.
- Next row: k2tog, K1, ssk.
- Next row: s1, k2tog, psso.
- Break yarn leaving a long tail, pull through remaining st.

Using the crochet hook, crochet a 2-cm (¾-in) chain (see page 19) with the starting tail of yarn.

Thread the tail at the tip of the beard up through the side of the beard to the top and make a matching chain for the second sideburn. Sew the beard in place around the face, using the photograph as a guide.

Robe

Make 2 identical pieces for the front and back. The pieces are knitted from the bottom to the top edge.

- Cast on 22 sts in pale pink.
- K 4 rows.
- Break yarn and join variegated yarn.
- Work 8 rows in st st, beg with a K row.
- Next row: K2, k2tog, K to last 4 sts, ssk, K2.
- Next row: P.
- Next row: K.
- Next row: P.
- Repeat last 4 rows twice more. [16 sts]
- Work 8 rows in st st, beg with a K row.
- Mark beg and end of last row with a piece of contrasting yarn or thread.
- Work 10 rows in st st, beg with a K row.
- Next row: Cast off 2 sts, K to end.
- Repeat last row once more. [12 sts]
- Cast off.

Seam the robe pieces together 2 sts along at each side of the neck opening to form shoulder seams.

For the sleeves, spread the two robe pieces apart. With the right side of your work facing you, pick up and K 16 sts between the two thread markers.

- Work 11 rows in st st, beg with a P row.
- Next row: K2, m1, K to last 2 sts, m1, K2.
- Next row: P.
- Repeat last 2 rows twice more. [22 sts]
- Break yarn and join pale pink yarn.
- K 2 rows.
- Cast off loosely.

Complete the second sleeve in exactly the same way. Remove the thread markers.

To make up, join the underarm and side seams.

Belt

Use the crochet hook and bright pink yarn to crochet a chain (see page 19), 35 cm (14 in) long. Sew the tails of the chain back through the chain. Wrap the belt twice around the wise man's waist and secure in a loose knot.

Wrap

- Cast on 7 sts in aqua.
- Work in st st until the wrap measures 22 cm (8¾ in).

Using gold crochet thread, work a single crochet border around the wrap as described on page 19.

Hat

- Cast on 30 sts in emerald green.
- Work 14 rows in st st, beg with a K row.
- Next row: (s1, k2tog, psso) 10 times. [10 sts]
- Next row: (p2tog) 5 times. [5 sts]
- Break yarn, thread it through the remaining sts, pull it up and secure.

To make up, sew back the seam. Roll up the lower edge to form a brim and secure at the back with a stitch. Sew a line of running stitches around the brim using gold crochet thread. Attach a sequin and a small button to the top of the hat.

Gifts

I chose to knit the wise men's gifts out of metallic embroidery thread, but you could also knit them from normal embroidery threads or fine wool. Use whatever thread colours, sequins and beads you have in your craft box.

The green package

- Cast on 18 sts in green.
- K 10 rows.
- Work 6 rows in st st, beg with a K row.
- Next row: (k2tog) 9 times. [9 sts]
- Break yarn, thread it through the remaining sts, pull it up and secure.

To make up, sew down the side seam, stuff fairly firmly and close the gap. Decorate the top with a sequin and a couple of beads.

The gold package

- Cast on 22 sts in gold.
- K 14 rows.
- Cast off.

To make up, fold in half widthways and oversew round the sides with the right side facing you. Stuff fairly firmly then close the gap and decorate the top with a fancy sequin.

The silver package

- Cast on 16 sts in silver.
- K 4 rows.
- Work 6 rows in st st, beg with a K row.
- Next row: (k2tog) 8 times. [8 sts]
- Work 5 rows in st st, beg with a P row.
- K 2 rows.
- Cast off.

To make up, oversew down the side seam with the right side facing you. Stuff fairly firmly then close the gap. Decorate the top with a few beads.

You will need

A small amount of bright yellow DK yarn

A large gold and small red sequin

Gold crochet thread for the hanging loop

A small amount of polyester toy stuffing

EQUIPMENT

A pair of 3 mm (US 2/3) knitting needles

A size 3.25 mm (US D-3) crochet hook

A yarn needle to sew the star together

Star

The star is knitted as two shapes that are sewn together and stuffed. If you like, you can add a hanging loop. I also used a couple of sequins for a bit of sparkle. You could add a button if you prefer or simply leave it plain.

Make 2 identical pieces.

- Cast on 2 sts in bright yellow.
- K 1 row.
- Next row: Inc 1, K2.
- K 3 rows.
- Next row: K1, m1, K1, m1, K1.
- K 3 rows.
- Next row: K1, m1, K to last st, m1, K1.
- K 5 rows.
- Next row: Cast on 7 sts, K to end.

- Next row: Cast on 7 sts, K to last 2 sts, ssk. [20 sts]
- Next row: k2tog, K to last 2 sts, ssk.
- Repeat last row four times more. [10 sts]
- Next row: k2tog, K to end. [9 sts]
- Next row: Inc 1, K to last st, inc 1, K1.
- Repeat last row five times more. [21 sts]
- Next row: Cast off 7 sts, K to end.
- Repeat last row once more. [7 sts]
- K 2 rows.
- Next row: k2tog, K to last 2 sts, ssk.
- K 2 rows.
- Next row: k2tog, K1, ssk.
- K 2 rows.
- Next row: s1, k2tog, psso.
- Break yarn and pull through remaining st.

To make up, oversew the sides of the star together, stuffing as you go. Sew the sequins at the centre of the star.

For the hanging cord, use the crochet hook and gold crochet thread to crochet a chain (see page 19), 10 cm (4 in) long. Thread the ends of the chain through the top of the star and secure.

Gifts for the King

Caspar, Melchior and Balthasar had to travel for many days and nights before they realized that the star was shining over the little town of Bethlehem, which was near Jerusalem. It was daytime when they entered the town and they couldn't see the star very clearly against the blue of the sky. They asked people in the street, *"Do you know where the new king has been born?"* but no one could help them.

Then, as darkness fell, they saw the star shining bright above a little stable, and they made their way there. As soon as they saw the baby Jesus lying asleep in a manger, they knelt down before him and worshipped him.

One by one they handed Mary their gifts for him. Caspar gave him gold, a gift that in those days was given only to kings. Melchior gave him frankincense, a beautiful-smelling incense that was used by priests in temples. And Balthasar gave him myrrh, a very rare and expensive kind of perfumed oil. These were gifts suitable not just for a king but for a god – or for the Son of God.

Mary thanked them for the gifts. The wise men stayed for a while to marvel at the special baby they had come all that way to find. They knew that something important had changed in the world the moment he was born. Nothing would ever be quite the same again. God had given the world his only son, and that is the most precious gift anyone can ever give.

Today we remember the three wise men and the gifts they gave to the baby Jesus, and that is why we give presents to each other at Christmas time. Around the world, more than two thousand years later, people still celebrate the day the holy child was born.

Creating your own Knitivity scene

Once you've knitted some of the figures in this book, you'll be ready to create your own Knitivity scene. Inside the back cover of this book you will find a piece of card with a manger that you can assemble very easily, and a backdrop. You may also wish to put the dolls in specific poses using wire or thread.

Assembling the backdrop

Using a pair of scissors, carefully cut off the whole of the section of card containing the manger so that you're left with just the backdrop. The backdrop can now be used as it is, but you may prefer to open up the doors (this adds stability as well as looks more interesting). To do this, cut around the top of the wooden door between the top two hinges, then cut down the middle between the two doors.

Score the folds using a butter knife and a straight edge to steady the knife blade and make a straight line. Carefully run the knife from the top of one hinge to the base of the door frame, then repeat on the opposite side. The doors should now open easily.

Assembling the manger

Using a pair of scissors, cut out the legs and the body of the manger.

To assemble the body of the manger, score along the folds using a butter knife and a straightedge, then use a small quantity of white glue to stick the tabs to the inside (figure a, opposite).

For each pair of legs, carefully cut twice along the yellow lines, then use a butter knife and a straight edge to score along the blue lines that indicate where you need to fold the template. Fold each leg, then use a small quantity of white glue to stick the grey tab to the back of each (figure b). You may need to hold the pieces together while the glue sets.

The backdrop

fold   cut   fold

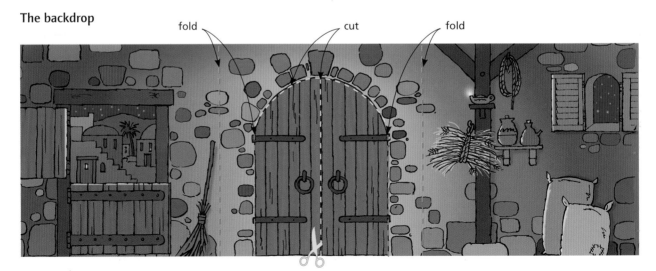

The manger

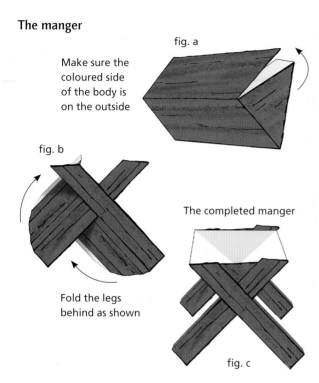

fig. a

Make sure the coloured side of the body is on the outside

fig. b

Fold the legs behind as shown

The completed manger

fig. c

Finally, stick the leg pairs to each end of the manger. Make sure that you match the position of each pair of legs so that all four legs touch the ground when you stand the manger up (figure c).

Creating shapes with wire and thread

The knitted dolls are quite soft. The figures will stand up, but you may wish to pose them so that Mary is holding Baby Jesus, or the Wise Men are pointing at the Star.

One method for doing this is to use PVC-covered garden wire. Cut a strip of wire approximately 12.5–14 cm (5–5½ in) long. Hold the figure's arms out so that there is a straight line from one hand to the other, then carefully thread the wire through the sleeves. You can guide the wire through using your fingers poked inside the neck of the figure's tunic or top.

You may also wish to have the dolls clasping their hands. To stitch the hands together, use a needle and some thread that is close in colour to the yarn you used to create the basic doll. Make sure you don't pull the thread too tight, otherwise it may be difficult to remove the thread later without damaging your knitting.

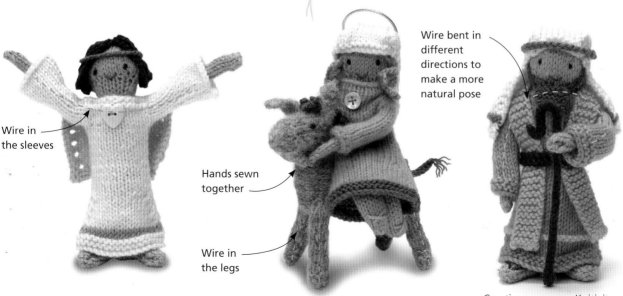

Wire in the sleeves

Wire bent in different directions to make a more natural pose

Hands sewn together

Wire in the legs

Index